Easy Camping Recipes

Foil Packet – Campfire Cooking – Grilling – Dutch Oven

Louise Davidson

Contents

Introduction

Any time is as good a time as any to go on a camping trip. Whether it's during a summer vacation or just a quick weekend getaway, a great night under the stars is worth it. All you'll need are camping gear and good company—although if you want to camp out by yourself, no one's stopping you. But if there's one thing a camping trip wouldn't be complete without, it's delicious camping food. This cookbook is here to help you with just that. In it you'll find an array of incredible recipes—from breakfast meals to quick snacks to desserts. You'll also be well informed about the ingredients you'll be needing, the equipment you'll be using, as well as the ways in how to cook all types of delicious camping food. But, before anything, I bet you're probably asking yourself this question: "Why should I even go camping?"

Camping can be a joyful experience, shared with friends and families alike. Being in the great outdoors brings people together, especially without the distractions of day-to-day affairs like work, cell phones, and the internet. Without these disturbances, families and friends can bond over hiking, swimming, games, and especially, food! The meal, the breaking of bread, is a time to come together and talk, to interact with each other in a way that our busy lives so often keep us from experiencing.

Family meals are important experiences to share. Magic can happen around the campfire when you're cooking and sharing great meals and stories together. Since none of these methods are regularly used at home, the many variations of camp cooking make the experience all the more unique. BBQ over a campfire, using coals, foil packet cooking, and more are all included in this cookbook!

Safety around the Fire and Cooking in the Outdoors

Much of the cooking within this book refers to open-flame style of cooking.

Fire safety is essential. Always keep an eye on the fire, never leave it unattended, and make sure that the fire is completely out, even if it is in a fire ring. Keep fire extinguishers at the ready, just in case.

Second, fire cooking is a tricky business. Until you know how to judge the heat of a fire or its coals, you may have some challenges first. The best way to attain success is to keep vigilant while cooking. Note that the best way to cook is directly on hot coals. This means you must have the time to start a fire, make it hot, and then let it die down into coals. If you do not have this time or patience, you might want to consider alternatives, as cooking over a flame though good, is trickier. Using a grill is helpful, and moving the food consistently may help prevent scorching. If you do not feel comfortable cooking over open flame, any camp stove will work quite well.

Do not forget to put the fire out after you are finished using it. One of the best ways to do this is to cover it with sand or dirt until it dies off completely.

Here are some additional tips regarding food safety. While this list is by no mean exhaustive, it is a good starting point.

- Washing your hands before and after handling food is an important safety rule to follow at all times. It may be even more so when cooking in the outside. You can also us hands sanitizers.

- Working on a clean surface, and keeping bugs and undesired creepy crawlers out of your food supply is also vital to avoid food poisoning. If you can, keeping your cooler in your car or trailer is a really good way to avoid contamination.

- Wash your fruits and vegetables with safe, drinkable water.

- Drink bottle you've bought or brought from home to make sure the water supply you use is safe to drink.

- Clean-up immediately after each meal, storing leftover food in airtight containers and away from night prowlers.

Food Security

All that said, special care should be taken when preparing your foods on site. Many of these recipes include foods that require refrigeration. Keep all foods in a cooler filled with ice or in a refrigerator until cooking. This is especially true for raw meats, dairy, and eggs. When preparing raw meats (and eggs), be careful not to cross-contaminate. This is when raw meat juices spread to other foods, like vegetables, which may be left raw. This is a problem because botulism and other bacteria can cause serious illness when consumed, even in small quantities. Make sure to wash hands, knives, and prep materials between each dish. Keeping a cutting board and knives for each food item (green for vegetables, white for meat, for example) can help prevent cross contamination. You may wish to prepare as much as possible prior to your camping trip.

Some Essentials to Bring on Your Trip:

For the fire

Waterproof matches or a few good lighters

Starter liquid fluid

Starter wood

Charcoals (plenty of it)

Cooking utensils for barbecue: tongs, spatula, extra-long forks, cleaning brush for the grill.

Grill (for over the fire, if the campsite does not provide or you like having your own)

A grate to place directly on the fire to cook food on the open flame

To prepare and cook the food

Large cast iron skillet or metal skillet that can be placed on the grill or fire

Saucepan

Heavy duty aluminum foil

Cooking spray of your choice.

Olive oil, butter

Salt and pepper and other seasoning you may want to use, like garlic powder, chili powder, and other spices.

Oven mitts (preferably silicone to accommodate very high temperatures)

Can opener

Bottle opener

Prepping knifes, cutting board

Whisk, spoons, wooden spoon, slotted spoon

Grater, vegetable peeler

Plastic strainer

Large unbreakable serving plates

Mixing bowl, various size

Measuring cups and spoons

Wood skewers

Zip lock bags

Mason jars – great for mixing dressings and has many other uses

To keep the food

One cooler with plenty of ice or ice packs to keep perishable food and drinks fresh

A second cooler or large plastic covered bin for dry non-perishable item like cans, pasta, rice, cereals, seasoning & spices.

Plastic wrap

Plastic airtight containers for food leftover storage

To eat

Non-breakable plates, glass, cups, mugs, utensils

Napkins

Plastic tablecloth

Water bottles

To clean-up

Paper towels

Washing clothes, drying clothes

Dish washing tub, dish washing soap

Common Tools and Preparations to Cook in the Great Outdoors

Knowing before you leave which cooking tools that you'll be needing is an important to make your next camping trip more enjoyable. Again, the simple and more versatile, the better. You're going to want tools that you can use again and again for different types of meals. Bringing a bunch of tools that you're only going to use maybe once or twice just isn't practical. So, choose wisely. Here are a few common tools that you'll be needing for your camping trip:

a) Dutch Oven

This is probably one of the most versatile camping tools there is. You can line this vessel with aluminum foil or just coat some oil on the bottom and sides before adding your ingredients. Using a Dutch oven is an ingenious way that allows you to bake without an oven. All you have to do is heat up some coals, then form a circle with them that's about the same circumference of your Dutch oven. Next, place the vessel over the hot coals. Put on the lid, add a few more hot coals on top, and voila! You're baking without gas or electricity. Aside from baking, you can also use a Dutch oven to boil and roast over the campfire.

b) Cast Iron Skillet

This vessel is a very helpful tool when it comes to cooking outdoors. A lot of campers opt to use a cast iron skillet because of its durability and its ability to preserve heat. Aside from this, you won't have to use a lot of oil because of its natural non-stick properties. Because of this, it's also a lot easier to clean because the cooked food slides right off. This vessel is great for fried meals cooked over the campfire, hot coals, or a portable camping stove.

c) Cast Iron Camp Cooker

Otherwise known as a Pie Cooker, this is a handy tool to have when you want to toast sandwiches or cook pretty much anything that includes bread or dough plus toppings or fillings. Its long handle makes it convenient to cook these types of meals over the campfire without worrying about being too close to the fire or burning yourself. Aside from this, you won't have to worry about spills or ingredients oozing out of the vessel since it's sealed tightly when closed. You can also rest easy knowing that your sandwich or pie will cook evenly with a camp cooker.

d) Tin Foil

Honestly, some meals don't even require any sort of cooking vessel. Sometimes all you'll need is a few large sheets of heavy-duty aluminum foil. Lay them flat on a surface and arrange your ingredients in the center. Next, bring the edges of the foil to the center and roll them together to seal. You can either cook them over or in the campfire, or on the grill. Using tin foil is great because you don't necessarily have to use plates or bowls to serve your cooked meals. You can eat your cooked meal directly from the foil packet. Afterward, you can just toss them in the trash. That's a lot less cleaning up to do. Who doesn't love that?

e) Wooden or metal skewers

If you're planning on making kebabs or S 'mores, you're going to need a few skewers. Alternate your ingredients onto each skewer and cook them over the campfire. Don't forget to rotate them constantly, so they'll be cooked evenly. You can also use sticks or wooden dowels to create a few desserts. You can whip up a delicious éclair with a wooden dowel by wrapping the crescent roll dough around the dowel and toasting it over an open fire. After a few minutes, you've got a cooked roll which you can squeeze custard or pudding into, then top with chocolate syrup and whipped cream. Yum!

f) Direct heat, Grill, and Portable Camping Stove

Although it isn't necessary to bring all of these items with you on your next camping trip, it's good to have at least one or two. Of course, the direct heat, which is simply your campfire fuelled by either firewood or hot coals, is a no-brainer. You're pretty much set for campfire cooking once you've prepared it. But it's handy to have either a grill or a portable camping stove with you, too. They're great for when you need a heat source that's easy to measure temperature since they're easier to adjust compared to using a campfire. And, obviously, they're a lot more convenient to set up.

Prep Early to Make Camping More Fun

You can make cooking at the campsite even easier on yourself by doing some of the food prep at home. Plastic food storage bags with secure closures are great for carrying premade ingredients in. They can be washable or disposable depending on your preference, they can easily be labeled, and they are the most compact way of storing food in small spaces.

When preparing food at home for the campsite, you have a couple of different options. With some dishes, you can prepare all of the ingredients and combine them together in one container so that all you need to do is transfer them from the container they will be cooked in. If you find that many of the dishes that you plan on preparing use the same ingredients, you can prepare larger quantities of those ingredients and store them in a plastic bag, retrieving only what you need at any given time. You can also prepare each set of ingredients for dishes separately, bag and label it, and then assemble it at the campsite.

When camping, you don't have to give up homemade flavor in favor of convenience foods. However certain premade, canned, and frozen foods not only save you time, but can also be easily enhanced with just a few small additions. For example, a jarred sauce with the addition of a few spices will taste heavenly and save you the extra time and ingredients of creating it from scratch.

Always pack a little extra. You never know when you will want seconds or meet a new mouth to feed. Welcome others into your campsite and make new friends and memories around your cast iron Dutch oven.

Cooking Techniques

Foil Packets

Cooking techniques while camping are unique. Aluminum foil packets are one of the most common methods included in the recipes. It consists of placing the food on an aluminum foil sheet and folding it tightly. The trick to foil packets is to keep the center seam at the top. This allows easy checking on the progress of the food, but also makes eating out of the pouch itself an easy possibility. They provide easy clean-up, with the fact that it is cook pot and serving dish all in one. Also, when cooking with foil packets you should not place the foil packets directly into the fire. Place them on a grill over the fire or on the coals once the fire dies down.

Open flames versus grilling

Certain recipes work well for cooking directly over the fire. S'Mores, foods that require boiling, and recipes that need charring do best over direct flame. However, most foods will cook best either on the grill (at a safe distance from direct flames) or on coals. Foil packets, for example, cook very well on hot coals. If you do cook directly on the grill, make sure the grill has been both cleaned and oiled.

Cooking with a Cast Iron Dutch Oven at the Campsite

When using a cast iron Dutch oven at your campsite, you will usually be applying heat to both the top and the bottom by means of charcoal briquettes. The recipes in this book assume a temperature of approximately 350°F. In order to achieve this, you will use briquettes in numbers that are proportional to the size of your oven. A general rule is to use twice as many briquettes as the diameter of your oven. So for example, if you have a 12-inch oven, you will use 24 pieces of charcoal. A 16-inch oven would require approximately 32. This of course is a very generalized rule that should only serve as a guideline. Always use a thermometer when you are learning to gauge the temperature of your oven, especially if you are using wood rather than coals.

The method of cooking is going to help determine where you place the coals and in what numbers. What this does is help you to distribute the heat at the area where it needs to be most concentrated or distributed. If you are any sautéing, boiling, frying, or open lid cooking, you will place the entire quantity of the coals underneath the oven. For methods of cooking that require both a top and bottom heat source, distribute the coal between the bottom and on top of the lid. Depending on the proportion of heat that you need from each heat source, divide them up with half on top and half on the bottom, or ¾ on the bottom and ¼ on top. Give yourself a little room to practice with adjusting the heat on your Dutch oven before creating more involved meals.

Cooking with your Dutch oven outside is a little different than using it indoors and requires just a few pieces of additional equipment. First of all, you definitely want a good, reliable lid lifting device. Cast iron can be very hot, especially if you have hot coals placed on the lid. To best protect yourself from burns, use a heat protective glove or mitt along with a lid lifting device to remove the lid from the oven. A lid stand is also a good idea. This will provide a heat-proof surface for your lid without setting it on the dirty ground. You may also find a long pair of tongs helpful for moving hot coal briquettes. If you spend a great deal of time cooking in the great outdoors, at some point you may wish to invest in either a tripod or a Dutch oven cooking table. Both of these devices are a little more cumbersome that just the Dutch oven, but they provide a more stable, safer cooking environment to work in.

Camp Food Hacks

So, part of the fun of cooking in the great outdoors is getting inventive. If you're a frequent camper, then you've definitely had to fashion cutlery or utensils out of some very strange things at one point or another.

Check out some of the following camp food hacks you can try out on your next camping trip:

- Instead of having your bread squished up among all the other things you're taking with you camping, keep it in a large, clean, tin can. Open it up at the site and enjoy non-squished-bread sandwiches. You can use any recipe you like for the baking of the bread.

- Freeze your water supply in large containers that you can place inside your cooler. They will keep the cooler cold and can be used for drinking water later.

- As an alternative to bread, take tortilla flour wraps. They take up less space than bread and can be used to make wraps, thin pizzas, and can even be crisped up for some chip-like action with salsa.

- Take salsa! Salsa is so versatile and will bring a new layer of flavor to your camping meals. It can be used in a ton of ways including as a dip, pasta sauce, in a stew, on tacos, on hot dogs – the choices are endless.

- Cooking meats and veggies with your basic salt and black pepper is alright if you're camping for just a day or two, but if you plan on trying out the recipes in this book, you will want to take along some other spices. A great way to make your spices portable is to store small amounts in Tic-Tac boxes.

- If you live somewhere where you can get some birch bark, grab some of that easy-burning fuel, bag it, and take it with you for starting campfires in a flash.

- You can make a portable grill with an aluminum tray filled with hot coals with a rack placed on top.

- When cooking burgers over a fire, place an ice cube on each burger and you will avoid drying out the inside of the burger.

Breakfast Recipes

Delicious Homemade French Toast for Camping

Enjoy this campfire-cooked sweet breakfast treat in just 45 minutes.

Serves: 6 – Preparation Time: 5 minutes – Cooking Time: 40 minutes

Nutritional facts per serving: calories 323, total fat 8 g, saturated fat 2 g, carbs 50 g, sugar 21 g, fibers 4 g, protein 13 g, sodium 393 mg

Ingredients

1 loaf bread, sliced

4 eggs

1⅓ cups milk

½ teaspoon ground cinnamon

2 teaspoons vanilla extract

Salt, to taste

¼ cup sliced almonds

½ pound fresh strawberries, washed and diced

½ pound fresh strawberries, washed and sliced

Powdered sugar, to taste

Maple syrup, to taste

Preparation

1. Prepare the French toast batter by combining eggs, milk, cinnamon, vanilla extract, and salt in a bowl. Mix well and set aside.

2. Cover bread loaf with parchment paper, leaving only the top part exposed. Then, wrap loosely in aluminum foil so that the slices aren't so close together.

3. Top bread loaf with diced strawberries. Sprinkle on top and in between slices. Then, do the same with the almonds.

4. Secure the parchment and foil around the loaf so that they have a tighter grip on the bread. Then, pour the prepared French toast batter on top. Coat entire loaf evenly. Afterwards, cover top with foil.

5. Cook over the campfire for about 35 to 40 minutes, depending on the intensity of the fire. Move the loaf around a bit to cook it evenly. The bread is ready once it is no longer soggy.

6. Allow to cool for about 10 minutes. Serve with powdered sugar, syrup, and remaining strawberries.

Easy Camp Cooker Ham 'n Egg Sandwich

Munch on this hassle-free breakfast sandwich in just 10 minutes using only 7 simple ingredients.

Serves: 2 – Preparation Time: 5 minutes – Cooking Time: 5 minutes

Nutritional facts per serving: calories 766, total fat 62 g, saturated fat 36 g, carbs 32 g, sugar 4 g, fibers 2 g, protein 21 g, sodium 1209 mg

Ingredients

2 eggs

Salt and pepper, to taste

1 stick butter, softened

4 slices bread

¼ cup cheddar cheese, grated

2 slices ham

Preparation

1. In a bowl, add eggs, salt, and pepper. Beat until smooth.

2. Spread butter on one side of each bread slice.

3. Layer bread, with butter facing outside, egg, cheese, ham, and another bread slice, with butter facing outside, into a camp cooker. Close, then cook over the campfire for about 5 minutes until toasted.

4. Repeat for the remaining sandwiches.

5. Serve.

Campfire-style 25-minute Beer Pancakes

Have some leftover beer from the night before? Put it to good use in these hearty and tasty beer-infused pancakes.

Serves: 16 – Preparation Time: 20 minutes – Cooking Time: 5 minutes

Nutritional facts per serving: calories 144, total fat 8 g, saturated fat 3 g, carbs 15 g, sugar 6 g, fibers 1 g, protein 3 g, sodium 165 mg

Ingredients

3⅓ pancake mix

½ cup toasted pine nuts

½ cup currants

2 cups pale lager beer

2 large eggs

¼ cup vegetable oil, plus more for cooking

Butter

Pancake syrup

Preparation

1. In a bowl, add pancake mix, nuts, and currants. Mix well until combined. Then, form a hole in the middle of the mixture. Pour in beer, eggs, and vegetable oil. Combine until incorporated.

2. Place a grilling grate on top of campfire, then put a cast iron pan on top to heat through. Test the hotness by dropping a few cold water droplets onto the pan. If sputtering, the pan is hot enough.

3. Pour in 1 tablespoon oil to coat pan, then pour ¼ cup pancake batter. Cook for about 3 to 4 minutes or until bubbles form on surface. Flip, then cook for another minute. Repeat for remaining batter.

4. Serve with butter and syrup drizzled on top.

Campfire Ham and Egg Breakfast Burritos

Whether you make these ahead or make them right away, these will surely make a delicious start to your day.

Serves: 8 – Preparation Time: 15 minutes – Cooking Time: 30 minutes

Nutritional facts per serving: calories 736, total fat 34 g, saturated fat 13 g, carbs 74 g, sugar 2 g, fibers 4 g, protein 32 g, sodium 1483 mg

Ingredients

½ tablespoon olive oil

1 cup frozen hash browns

8 ounces cooked ham, chopped

12 eggs

1 tablespoon taco seasoning

1 4½-ounce canned green chilies

2 cups cheddar cheese, grated

¼ cup cilantro, diced

8 12-inch flour tortillas

Preparation

1. In a pan, heat olive oil. Stir fry hash browns in pan for about one minute, then toss in ham. Cook for about 8 to 10 minutes or until both ingredients have browned.

2. As hash browns and ham cook, beat eggs in a large bowl then mix in taco seasoning.

3. Add egg and taco seasoning mixture into pan with browned hash browns and ham. Stir to scramble the eggs a few times. Once eggs are cooked mix in green chilies, cheese, and cilantro.

4. To make the burritos, spread about ⅛ cooked egg mixture along the center of the tortilla, forming a line. Fold in and around like a burrito then cover tightly in aluminum foil. Repeat for remaining tortillas.

5. To heat, arrange burritos on hot coals near fire. Cook for about 5 minutes, turn, then cook for another 5 minutes or longer depending on the intensity of your fire.

6. Serve.

Crispy Campfire-cooked Bacon

This amazing technique could change the way you cook bacon strips during camping trips forever.

Serves: 2 – Preparation Time: 1 minute – Cooking Time: 30 minutes

Nutritional facts per serving: calories 81, total fat 9 g, saturated fat 3 g, carbs 1 g, sugar 1 g, fibers 0 g, protein 6 g, sodium 320 mg

Ingredients

4 strips bacon

Preparation

1. Loosely fold bacon strips into a skewer. You can fit as many as you can on each skewer until you only have about 3 inches left of skewer remaining at the end.

2. Place two logs or bricks on opposite sides of your campfire. Then, position the skewers so that the ends are resting on the supports while the bacon cooks over the fire.

3. Cook for about 30 minutes, rotating every 5 minutes to make sure that each strip cooks evenly.

4. Serve.

Hash Brown Breakfast Pizza for Camping

Grill this delicious breakfast in 40 minutes after a 15-minute ingredient preparation with your family. This one's sure to be a crowd favorite.

Serves: 6 – Preparation Time: 15 minutes – Cooking Time: 40 minutes

Nutritional facts per serving: calories 461, total fat 31 g, saturated fat 15 g, carbs 25 g, sugar 1 g, fibers 0 g, protein 23 g, sodium 959 mg

Ingredients

4 cups hash browns, shredded
8 eggs, divided
1 teaspoon seasoning salt
1 cup cooked ham, diced
½ cup mushrooms, sliced
¼ cup scallions
¼ cup milk
1½ cups cheddar cheese, shredded

Preparation

1. Add hash browns in a bowl. Add 2 eggs and toss to coat. Add salt and combine. Set aside.

2. Line the bottom of a 12-inch cast iron skillet with hash brown mixture. Place onto camp grill and cover. Cook for about 10 minutes or until golden brown.

3. Add ham to a bowl. Mix in mushrooms, scallions, remaining eggs, milk, and cheese until well combined. Pour mixture over cooked hash brown crust.

4. Return to grill and cover with a lid or foil. Cook for about 10 to 15 minutes until eggs are done.

5. Slice and serve.

Sausage and Egg Camping Breakfast Burger

This scrumptious breakfast burger is created with made-from-scratch fluffy biscuits, deliciously savory sausage patties, and tasty sunny-side-up eggs.

Serves: 12 – Preparation Time: 15 minutes – Cooking Time: 25 minutes

Nutritional facts per serving: calories 446, total fat 33 g, saturated fat 11 g, carbs 22 g, sugar 1 g, fibers 1 g, protein 16 g, sodium 718 mg

Ingredients

2 cups flour

3 teaspoons baking powder

1 tablespoon sugar

1 teaspoon salt

6 tablespoons dry milk powder

2 teaspoons black pepper

4 tablespoons canola oil, plus more for frying

½ cup cheddar cheese, grated

1 cup water, plus 1 tablespoon

12 sausage patties

12 eggs

Salt and pepper

Ketchup, optional

Preparation

1. To make the biscuits, add flour, baking powder, sugar, salt, milk powder, pepper, and oil in a bowl. Mix well until fully combined. Pour ½ cup water. Add 1 tablespoon water, mixing afterwards. Keep adding until you have incorporated the remaining ½ cup water. Mix in grated cheese.

2. Heat a cast iron skillet over medium heat on your camping stove. Drizzle oil to coat. Pour about ¼ cup biscuit batter onto pan. Cook until lightly brown then turn. Cook remaining side until a bit thick and thoroughly cooked. Repeat for remaining batter. Wrap biscuits in foil to keep warm and set aside.

3. Wipe skillet clean and cook sausages over medium-high heat until lightly brown on each side and fully cooked. Remove from skillet, cover with foil to keep warm, and set aside.

4. Wipe skillet clean and cook eggs until cooked to your liking.

5. To assemble, cut biscuits in half. Add sausage and egg on top of bottom half. Season with salt and pepper. Drizzle ketchup on top if desired, then cover with top biscuit half. Repeat for remaining burgers.

6. Serve.

Raspberry Dutch Oven Pancake

This is a quick breakfast that is delicious and easy to make. Plus, it doesn't taste at all like your usual pancake—it's way better.

Serves: 6 – Preparation Time: 5 minutes – Cooking Time: 25 minutes

Nutritional facts per serving: calories 322, total fat 15 g, saturated fat 7 g, carbs 37 g, sugar 15 g, fibers 3 g, protein 10 g, sodium 349 mg

Ingredients

6 large eggs

1 cup flour

1 cup milk

1 teaspoon kosher salt

2 tablespoons sugar

¼ cup butter

2 cups raspberries, divided

Maple Syrup

Preparation

1. Prepare fire by heating about charcoal briquettes in a chimney starter for 15 minutes or until gray.

2. As briquettes heat up, mix eggs and flour in a bowl. Once smooth, add in milk, salt, and sugar. Mix well until combined.

3. Take a few hot briquettes and form a ring that is just a bit smaller than the width of your Dutch oven. Lay Dutch oven on top. Melt butter inside then spread across the bottom. Add prepared egg mixture then sprinkle 1½ cups raspberries over the mixture. Cover, then add some more hot briquettes on the lid. Cook for about 20 to 25 minutes until golden brown and set.

4. Sprinkle the rest of the raspberries on top of the pancake. Drizzle pancake syrup on top.

5. Serve.

Camping Sausage Pancake

Cooked over the campfire, this huge pancake is both fluffy and crisp with enough protein to start off your camping day right.

Serves: 4 – Preparation Time: 20 minutes – Cooking Time: 40 minutes

Nutritional facts per serving: calories 664, total fat 49 g, saturated fat 19 g, carbs 38 g, sugar 12 g, fibers 2 g, protein 22 g, sodium 1607 mg

Ingredients

½ cup fine-ground yellow cornmeal

½ cup all-purpose flour

1 tablespoon granulated sugar

¾ teaspoon fine salt

½ teaspoon baking powder

1 cup whole milk

2 large eggs

2 tablespoons unsalted butter

12 small breakfast sausage links, uncooked

3 tablespoons maple syrup, plus more for serving

Preparation

1. In a bowl, combine cornmeal, flour, sugar, salt, and baking powder. Pour in milk and eggs. Mix until incorporated.

2. Ready your campfire by placing a grilling grate on top. You want the heat to medium-high.

3. Heat a large cast iron pan on top of grate for about 5 minutes. Then, add butter and heat until bubbling. Toss in sausage and cook for about 12 to 15 minutes until well browned and thoroughly cooked. Remove from heat and transfer onto plate.

4. Mix the batter again just a little bit. Pour into pan from earlier. Make sure the batter is flat and even on the entire skillet. Then, return sausages into pan by distributing them evenly onto the batter. Add a drizzle of maple syrup on top of everything. Cover pan with foil. Allow to cook for 15 minutes or until pancake is lightly brown and thoroughly cooked.

5. Remove from heat and serve in wedges with additional maple syrup on the side.

Grilled Potato and Cheese Foil Packets

This is perfect for an easy breakfast to be enjoyed in the great outdoors. It's simple, easy to make, and super delicious!

Serves: 4 – Preparation Time: 15 minutes – Cooking Time: 35 minutes

Nutritional facts per serving: calories 449, total fat 19 g, saturated fat 12 g, carbs 47 g, sugar 3 g, fibers 7 g, protein 23 g, sodium 1146 mg

Ingredients

3 large potatoes, peeled and cut into small cubes

1 medium onion, chopped

3 tablespoons Parmesan cheese, shredded

1 tablespoon chives, finely chopped

½ teaspoon seasoned salt

¼ teaspoon pepper

2 tablespoons butter

½ cup bacon, crumbled and cooked

½ cup mozzarella cheese, grated

½ cup cheddar cheese, grated

Preparation

1. On a flat surface, prepare a double-layer of 18-inch sheets of aluminum foil.

2. Mix potatoes, onion, Parmesan, chives, salt, and pepper in a bowl. Then pour mixture onto the prepared foil. Distribute butter evenly on top.

3. Wrap mixture in foil by folding foil to the center and rolling the top to seal.

4. Place on camp grill over medium heat. Cover and cook for about 15 min on each side or until potatoes become soft.

5. Open foil carefully and distribute bacon, mozzarella, and cheddar cheese evenly on top. Seal packet again. Cook for 3 minutes or more, just enough for the cheese to melt.

6. Open foil again. Serve warm.

Scrambled Eggs with Bacon and Potatoes

This "farmer's breakfast" is meal that's fit for a king. Simple and delicious, this breakfast is a great way to give your fun and exciting camping day a good start.

Serves: 2 – Preparation Time: 15 minutes – Cooking Time: 30 minutes

Nutritional facts per serving: calories 875, total fat 29 g, saturated fat 10 g, carbs 118 g, sugar 8 g, fibers 15 g, protein 36 g, sodium 520 mg

Ingredients

6 medium cooked potatoes, cubed*

8 slices bacon, finely chopped

2 tablespoons butter

1 medium onion, diced

6 eggs

Salt and pepper, to taste

Parsley

Preparation

1. Cook bacon in a cast iron skillet over medium heat until crispy. Transfer to a plate lined with paper towels to drain. Retain bacon grease.

2. Add butter to the same pan, and then add onions. Sauté until fragrant and translucent, about 1-2 minutes. Add potatoes and cook until crisp. Chop bacon into small bits and back into pan.

3. Add eggs to a bowl and whisk well before adding them to the pan. Scramble eggs, making sure to include everything. Season with salt and pepper, to taste.

4. Remove from heat and transfer to a plate. Garnish with parsley on top to serve.

*Prepare potatoes at home before the camping trip. Store in an airtight container and place in the cooler until ready to use.

Campfire Cheese and Sausage Sandwich

This toasted sandwich is filled with a mixture of delicious melted and gooey American cheese and tasty, savory sausages.

Serves: 2 – Preparation Time: 2 minutes – Cooking Time: 8 minutes

Nutritional facts per serving: calories 504, total fat 34 g, saturated fat 16 g, carbs 25 g, sugar 3 g, fibers 1 g, protein 25 g, sodium 1012 mg

Ingredients

Non-stick cooking spray

4 slices bread

1 tablespoon butter

2 eggs

2 American cheese slices

2 sausage patties, cooked

Preparation

1. Coat inner sides of camp cooker with cooking spray.
2. Spread butter onto one side of each bread slice and transfer onto camp cooker with the buttered side facing down, one on each side.
3. Next, in a bowl, beat eggs. Distribute onto bread. Then, add cheese slices and sausage on top. Close camp cookers.
4. Toast over campfire for about 4 to 8 minutes, rotating every now and then to cook evenly.
5. Serve.

Spicy Crab Omelette

This breakfast dish has eggs, meat, and a few vegetables tossed in there to make it a complete and hearty meal. It has just a hint of spiciness and can be done in 25 minutes.

Serves: 2 – Preparation Time: 5 minutes – Cooking Time: 20 minutes

Nutritional facts per serving: calories 603, total fat 38 g, saturated fat 17 g, carbs 39 g, sugar 4 g, fibers 5 g, protein 26 g, sodium 343 mg

Ingredients

5 eggs

⅓ cup cream

½ teaspoon lemon zest

5 drops hot sauce

3 tablespoons cheddar cheese, grated

Salt and pepper, to taste

1 tablespoon oil

1 large potato, cut into small cubes

1 small onion, finely chopped

¼ cup red bell pepper, finely chopped

1 cup crabmeat, canned

Preparation

1. Prepare the charcoal and place grill above.

2. Combine eggs, cream, lemon zest, hot sauce, cheddar cheese, salt, and pepper in a bowl. Reserve for later.

3. Add oil to a Dutch oven and place over the grill. . Add potato and onion. Sauté until thoroughly cooked and potato browns. Then, toss in red pepper and cook until soft, 2-4 minutes.

4. Add reserved egg mixture into skillet and sprinkle crab meat evenly over top.

5. Cook for about 5 minutes or until eggs are just about to set. Place a lid on top. Add some hot coals on lid to lightly toast the top, 2-4 minutes.

6. Serve immediately.

Eggs and Bacon in a Bag

This simple 2-ingredient breakfast is super simple and delicious. It takes 10 minutes or less to make.

Serves: 1 – Preparation Time: 5 minutes – Cooking Time: 5 minutes

Nutritional facts per serving: calories 159, total fat 11 g, saturated fat 4 g, carbs 1 g, sugar 0 g, fibers 0 g, protein 13 g, sodium 434 mg

Ingredients

2 strips bacon, cut in half

1 egg

Salt and pepper, to taste

Preparation

1. Take a paper bag and arrange bacon strips on the bottom like a nest.
2. Crack open egg and add to bag. Season with salt and pepper, to taste.
3. Fold the top edges of paper bag twice and make a small hole using a knife through the folds. Insert a wooden stick through the hole.
4. Cook over campfire until bacon fat is melted and the egg is cooked through, being careful not too have the bag too close to the flames.
5. Remove from heat. Serve bag over a plate to prevent spillage.

Lunch Recipes

Campfire Chili and Cheese Macaroni

Don't be fooled by this pasta dish's simplicity—this one's packed with a delicious cheesy flavor paired with a tasty chili sauce.

Serves: 6 – Preparation Time: 1 minute – Cooking Time: 15 minutes

Nutritional facts per serving: calories 361, total fat 18 g, saturated fat 5 g, carbs 41 g, sugar 2 g, fibers 5 g, protein 11 g, sodium 663 mg

Ingredients

1 16-ounce box elbow macaroni

3 cups water

1 15-ounce can chili

1 7-ounce bag corn chips

½ cup cheddar cheese, grated

Preparation

1. In a large pan, boil pasta in water for about 10 minutes over high heat. Stir from time to time while cooking.
2. Once liquid is greatly reduced, pour in chili and let simmer.
3. Remove from heat. Scatter corn chips and cheese on top.
4. Serve.

Campfire Bacon and Cheese Potatoes

This bacon-cheese-potato combo makes a simple yet delicious and satisfying afternoon meal in the great outdoors.

Serves: 4 – Preparation Time: 10 minutes – Cooking Time: 45 minutes

Nutritional facts per serving: calories 441, total fat 17 g, saturated fat 9 g, carbs 54 g, sugar 3 g, fibers 6 g, protein 19 g, sodium 509 mg

Ingredients

8 strips bacon, chopped

3 large potatoes, sliced

Salt and pepper, to taste

2 onions, sliced

1 cup cheddar cheese, shredded

Preparation

1. Cook bacon in a Dutch oven. Once cooked, remove from vessel but leave the bacon grease inside. Set bacon pieces aside.

2. Spread potatoes in a single layer on the bottom of the Dutch oven. Season with salt and pepper. Then, add a single layer of onions followed by cheese and cooked bacon. Repeat each layer until you've used up all the ingredients.

3. Cook for about 45 minutes or until potatoes are tender.

4. Serve.

Hearty Campfire Lasagna

This warm, meaty, and cheese-filled pasta dish makes a great meal to be enjoyed with the entire family.

Serves: 8 – Preparation Time: 10 minutes – Cooking Time: 1 hour

Nutritional facts per serving: calories 845, total fat 53 g, saturated fat 25 g, carbs 43 g, sugar 3 g, fibers 4 g, protein 47 g, sodium 895 mg

Ingredients

15 lasagna noodles

2 pounds ground beef, browned and drained*

3 cups spaghetti sauce

3 cups mozzarella cheese, divided

2 cups ricotta cheese

½ cup Parmesan cheese, shredded

2 eggs

½ tablespoon dried basil

½ tablespoons dried oregano

1 14-ounce can artichoke hearts, drained and quartered

8 ounces fresh mushrooms, sliced

1 cups fresh spinach

1 cup water

Preparation

1. Light charcoal briquettes in a chimney starter for about 10 minutes or until gray and ashy.

2. Meanwhile, add lasagna noodles to the bottom of a 10-inch Dutch oven.

3. Top with ¼ of the ground beef and spaghetti sauce. In a bowl, mix 2 cups mozzarella, ricotta, parmesan, eggs, basil, and oregano.

4. Add ⅓ cheese and egg mixture on top. Scatter mushrooms, spinach, and artichoke hearts. Repeat until you've made three layers, with the last layer being the beef and spaghetti sauce mixture followed by remaining spinach.

5. Pour water over the top circling the outside edge of the lasagna. Cover.

6. Form a ring of hot briquettes, then lay Dutch oven on top. On the lid, place some more hot briquettes. Cook for 1 hour, scattering remaining 1 cup mozzarella on top during last 15 minutes of cooking.

7. Serve.

*It's a good idea to cook the ground beef at home before leaving on your trip. Store in an airtight container and refrigerate up to 4 days before using.

Campfire-style Roast Beef and Cheese Sandwich

This camp-friendly version of the classic Philly Cheesesteak sandwich is must-try for your next nature trip.

Serves: 6 – Preparation Time: 5 minutes – Cooking Time: 30 minutes

Nutritional facts per serving: calories 845, total fat 54 g, saturated fat 18 g, carbs 32 g, sugar 1 g, fibers 3 g, protein 55 g, sodium 1255 mg

Ingredients

2 tablespoons butter

3 bell peppers, sliced

1 onion, sliced

¼ cup oyster sauce

1 loaf French bread

¼ cup garlic butter

1⅓ pounds roast beef, sliced

1 pound provolone cheese, sliced

Non-stick cooking spray

Preparation

1. Light charcoal briquettes in a chimney starter for about 10 minutes or until gray and ashy.

2. In a pan, melt butter. Add peppers, onion, and oyster sauce. Stir fry until peppers are thoroughly cooked. Remove from heat and set aside.

3. Cut French bread into 1½-inch thick slices but only about ¾ through the bread.

4. Brush garlic butter onto the insides of each cut. Then, add a heaping spoonful of cooked pepper and onion mixture in between each slice followed by roast beef and provolone cheese.

5. Top with extra cheese.

6. Coat one side of aluminum foil with non-stick cooking spray so that the melted cheese won't stick to the inside of the foil. Then, wrap loaf, with oil-coated side inside, with foil. Make sure to wrap the entire loaf completely with foil. Use another sheet if necessary.

7. Put loaf beside hot coals, but not directly on the fire. Cook for about 30 minutes., turning sides a few times.

8. Serve.

Healthy Grilled Tofu and Eggplant Foil Packets

This vegetarian foil bundle is filled with an assortment of scrumptious veggies, making this a nutritious lunch for four.

Serves: 4 – Preparation Time: 10 minutes – Cooking Time: 10 minutes

Nutritional facts per serving: calories 356, total fat 30 g, saturated fat 4 g, carbs 13 g, sugar 8 g, fibers 5 g, protein 14 g, sodium 166 mg

Ingredients

20 ounces firm tofu, cut into 16 chunks

12 ounces eggplant, quartered lengthwise and cut into chunks

2 tablespoons ginger, finely chopped

2 tablespoons garlic, finely chopped

¼ cup soy sauce, plus more for serving

7 tablespoons vegetable oil, divided

2 scallions, sliced

1 cucumber, halved and cut into chunks

1 cup cilantro leaves

1 cup whole dill sprigs

1 red jalapeño pepper, halved and sliced

2 tablespoons lime juice

½ teaspoon kosher salt

Cooked rice

Preparation

1. In a large Ziploc bag, add tofu, eggplant, ginger, garlic, soy sauce, 5 tablespoons vegetable oil, and scallions. Seal tightly and massage using your hand to mix ingredients together. Store in a cooler to chill for about 1 hour.

2. When ready to cook, preheat camping grill to high at about 450 to 550 °F.

3. Lay flat 4 large sheets of aluminum foil and distribute tofu and eggplant mixture equally onto each. Fold sheets towards the center and seal edges.

4. Place foil packets onto grill and cook for about 5 minutes on each side. Remove from heat and set aside.

5. While packets are cooking, toss together cucumber, cilantro, dill, jalapeño, lime juice, remaining vegetable oil, and salt in a bowl.

6. Open up foil packets and scatter salad evenly onto each.

7. Serve with rice and soy sauce on the side.

Camping Vegetarian Pasta Foil Packets

This is a deliciously healthy pasta dish prepared with Roma tomatoes, fresh basil leaves, and goat cheese, all topped with a drizzle of fresh lemon juice. Yum!

Serves: 6 – Preparation Time: 15 minutes – Cooking Time: 10 minutes

Nutritional facts per serving: calories 224, total fat 11 g, saturated fat 4 g, carbs 20 g, sugar 9 g, fibers 5 g, protein 8 g, sodium 270 mg

Ingredients

1 pound spaghetti noodles, cooked according to package instructions

6 Roma tomatoes, seeded and dlced

1 cup fresh basil leaves, roughly chopped

½ teaspoon salt

¼ teaspoon ground pepper

3 garlic cloves, minced

3 tablespoons olive oil

1 lemon, cut into 6 wedges

4 ounces goat cheese

Preparation

1. Set camp grill to medium heat.

2. Mix pasta, tomatoes, basil, salt, pepper, garlic, and olive oil in a large bowl. Set aside.

3. Prepare 12 large sheets of aluminum foil. Place one on top of the other forming 6 double-layered sheets. Add about 1¼ pasta mixture onto the center of each sheet. Squeeze out lemon juice from lemon wedge over top of pasta then add lemon wedge to the mixture. Then, scatter about 2 to 3 teaspoons goat cheese on top of mixture. Close foil

packets by folding sheets to the center then rolling up the edges securely.

4. Cook foil packets on preheated grill over low heat for about 10 to 12 minutes. Shake packets once there is only about 5 or 6 minutes cooking time left.

5. Remove from heat. Serve.

Easy Campfire Pizza

Melted, gooey mozzarella, tasty pepperoni, and a delicious pizza sauce sandwiched in toasted pizza dough... What's not to love about this simple 15-minute pizza?

Serves: 4 – Preparation Time: 5 minutes – Cooking Time: 10 minutes

Nutritional facts per serving: calories 730, total fat 49 g, saturated fat 22 g, carbs 36 g, sugar 9 g, fibers 4 g, protein 36 g, sodium 2361 mg

Ingredients

1 14-ounce package pizza crust dough

Non-stick cooking spray

1 12-ounce package mozzarella cheese, grated

1 9-ounce package pepperoni, sliced

7½ ounces pizza sauce

Preparation

1. Roll out pizza dough, then cut into four equal rectangles.

2. Coat insides of camp cooker with non-stick cooking spray and transfer each rectangle onto camp cooker. Half of the rectangle should be on each side of the camp cooker. Next, spread pizza sauce on one half of dough then top with mozzarella and pepperoni. Repeat for remaining rectangles.

3. Close camp cooker and place over fire. Cook for about 5 to 10 minutes, depending on the intensity of your campfire. Keep turning camp cooker as pizza cooks. It is ready once pizza dough has browned.

4. Remove from heat. Serve.

Campfire Cheese and Veggies Quesadilla

Cooked over the campfire, this quesadilla makes a delicious and easy cheese-and-vegetable-packed lunch.

Serves: 4 – Preparation Time: 20 minutes – Cooking Time: 5 minutes

Nutritional facts per serving: calories 267, total fat 14 g, saturated fat 1 g, carbs 26 g, sugar 0 g, fibers 2 g, protein 12 g, sodium 428 mg

Ingredients

2 teaspoons canola oil

½ medium red onion, finely sliced

10 button mushrooms, finely sliced

½ cup corn

Salt and pepper, to taste

4 flour tortillas

1 cup pepper-jack cheese, grated

Preparation

1. In a cast iron skillet, add oil and heat over campfire. Once oil is hot, toss in onion and mushrooms. Stir fry until tender and a bit brown. Stir in corn and cook for another few minutes. Turn off heat. Season with salt and pepper.

2. Top 4 sheets of aluminum foil with a tortilla. In a straight line along the center, place equal amounts of cheese onto each tortilla followed by the cooked vegetables. Top with another layer of cheese. Seal tortilla by folding edges to the middle, then fold aluminum foil to the center to wrap tortilla. Roll edges of foil together to secure quesadillas.

3. Place a grilling grate on top of campfire then put foil wraps on top. Cook, turning once, until cheese has melted and tortillas are crispy and toasted, about 2-4 minutes.

Grilled Chicken, Chorizo, and Seafood Paella

This classic Spanish dish is perfect for a slightly fancier (but with hardly any effort) meal in the woods. This one's sure to impress friends and family.

Serves: 6 – Preparation Time: 20 minutes – Cooking Time: 45 minutes

Nutritional facts per serving: calories 682, total fat 24 g, saturated fat 8 g, carbs 77 g, sugar 2 g, fibers 3 g, protein 41 g, sodium 1474 mg

Ingredients

1 15-ounce can diced tomatoes

16 large shrimp, peeled and deveined

1 teaspoon paprika, divided

1 teaspoon salt, plus more for seasoning

Pepper, to taste

1 pound chicken thighs, boneless and skinless, chopped into bite-sized chunks

8 ounces Spanish chorizo, sliced ¼-inch-thick

1 to 2 tablespoons olive oil, if necessary

1 medium yellow onion, diced

2 medium cloves garlic, minced

1 large pinch saffron threads

2 cups Valencia rice

4 cups chicken broth

2 tablespoons parsley leaves, roughly chopped

Preparation

1. In a bowl, add chicken and shrimp. Season with ¼ teaspoon paprika and salt and pepper to taste. Toss to combine and coat. With tongs, separate chicken and shrimp and arrange on each side of the bowl. Store in a cooler until ready to use.

2. Preheat camping grill to high at about 450 to 550°F. Then, put a large paella pan onto grill and heat, covered, for about 1-2 minutes.

3. Once pan is hot, add chorizo. Cook chorizo for about 2 minutes or until browned, stirring occasionally. Move chorizo to a plate using tongs. Set aside.

4. In the same pan, you will notice that a layer of fat from the chorizo has formed on the bottom. If there is too little, feel free to add about 1 to 2 tablespoons olive oil. Next, add prepared chicken from earlier and cook, stirring from time to time, for about 6 minutes or until lightly brown.

5. Remove cooked chicken from pan then move to the same bowl as cooked chorizo. Set aside.

6. Return pan to heat and add onion. Sprinkle salt and pepper to season. Cook onion for about 5 minutes until tender. Mix in garlic, remaining paprika, and saffron. Cook for 30 seconds more.

7. Add tomatoes pour into pan and cook for about 3 minutes until color darkens. Scrape any toasted bits off the bottom of pan. Toss in rice and 1 teaspoon salt to mix with tomato and other ingredients.

8. Pour in broth to pan, then mix with other ingredients. Slightly flatten rice to form a somewhat smooth layer. Scatter cooked chorizo and chicken on top.

9. Let simmer for 12-15 minutes until liquid has been greatly reduced and rice is cooked.

10. Next, add prepared shrimp into rice. Create a bit of a pocket for them into the rice. Cook for 5-10 minutes more until shrimp have turned pink.

11. Remove pan from heat. Place a foil on top to cover and set aside for 5 minutes.

12. Remove foil and season dish with parley.

Toasted Chocolate, Peanut Butter, and Banana Sandwich

Made with deliciously sweet ingredients sandwiched in two toasted white bread slices, this meal is perfect for someone who's craving for a mixture of dessert and lunch.

Serves: 1 – Preparation Time: 2 minutes – Cooking Time: 6 minutes

Nutritional facts per serving: calories 598, total fat 34 g, saturated fat 14 g, carbs 67 g, sugar 28 g, fibers 6 g, protein 14 g, sodium 476 mg

Ingredients

2 slices white bread

1 tablespoon semisweet chocolate chips

2 tablespoons peanut butter

1 banana, sliced

1 tablespoon butter

Preparation

1. Spread peanut butter onto one side of each bread slice. Layer chocolate chips onto one slice on top of the peanut butter, then the sliced banana on the second slice on top of the peanut butter.

2. Close sandwiches together, layers facing inward. Coat outer bread slices with butter.

3. Add sandwich to camp cooker. Close, then cook over campfire for about 5 minutes or more, depending on the heat of the fire, until chips melts and bread is nice and toasted.

4. Serve.

Camp Cooker Tacos

This 15-minute taco makes a great camp-friendly afternoon meal that both kids and kids-at-heart will enjoy.

Serves: 6 – Preparation Time: 5 minutes – Cooking Time: 10 minutes

Nutritional facts per serving: calories 282, total fat 17 g, saturated fat 7 g, carbs 21 g, sugar 1 g, fibers 2 g, protein 12 g, sodium 382 mg

Ingredients

1 pound lean ground beef

1 ounce package taco seasoning mix

½ cup water

Non-stick cooking spray

12 6-inch tortillas

1 cup cheddar cheese, grated

½ cup onion

1 cup lettuce, grated

1 cup tomatoes, chopped

1 cup salsa

1 cup sour cream

Preparation

1. In a large pan, cook ground beef over medium-high heat until browned.

2. Add taco seasoning and mix well. Add water and cook until the water has evaporated.

3. Coat insides of camp cooker with non-stick cooking spray and lay tortilla flat inside. Then, spoon about ¼ cup cooked beef onto the center of tortilla. Add cheese and onion on

top. Place another tortilla on top of filling. Close camp cooker. Repeat for remaining tacos.

4. Heat tortilla on top of coals for about 10 minutes. Remove from camp cooker and top with lettuce, tomatoes, salsa and sour cream to serve.

Grilled Sausage and Veggie Packs

Cooked on the grill while wrapped in aluminum foil, this is a hearty and delicious lunch that's perfect for the entire family. No clean up necessary, either!

Serves: 4 – Preparation Time: 10 minutes – Cooking Time: 20 minutes

Nutritional facts per serving: calories 426, total fat 21 g, saturated fat 10 g, carbs 34 g, sugar 8 g, fibers 7 g, protein 27 g, sodium 1221 mg

Ingredients

1 12.8-ounce package smoked sausage, finely sliced

1 pound baby red potatoes, cut into quarters

1 pound green beans, trimmed

8 ounces white mushrooms, cut in half

1 onion, diced

4 tablespoons unsalted butter, divided

4 teaspoons Cajun seasoning, divided

Salt and pepper, to taste

2 tablespoons fresh parsley leaves, diced

Preparation

1. Set camp grill to high heat.

2. On a flat surface, prepare 4 12-inch long sheet of aluminum foil. Evenly distribute sausage, potatoes, green beans, mushrooms, and onion onto the center of each sheet.

3. Roll up each side of the 4 packets to shape them into bowls. Then, add butter, Cajun seasoning, salt, and pepper. Lightly toss together to mix.

4. Roll all sides of each packet towards their centers and seal on top with a few folds.

5. Transfer packets to preheated grill and cook for about 12 to 15 minutes until thoroughly cooked.

6. Carefully, open up packets and sprinkle parsley on top. Serve.

Mexican-inspired Chicken and Veggies Foil Packet

Wrapped in aluminum foil and cooked over the grill, this spicy Mexican-inspired dish is packed with yummy chicken and vegetables, making it as delicious as it is hearty.

Serves: 4 – Preparation Time: 5 minutes – Cooking Time: 25 minutes

Nutritional facts per serving: calories 276, total fat 6 g, saturated fat 1 g, carbs 15 g, sugar 1 g, fibers 4 g, protein 41 g, sodium 718 mg

Ingredients

2 tablespoons chili powder

2 tablespoons cumin

1 teaspoon garlic powder

1 teaspoon onion powder

1 teaspoon salt

1½ pounds chicken breasts, boneless and skinless, cut into strips

1 red bell pepper, cut into strips

1 green bell pepper, cut into strips

1 yellow bell pepper, cut into strips

1 red onion, cut into strips

Preparation

1. In a bowl, add chili powder, cumin, garlic powder, onion powder, and salt. Mix until incorporated. Then, add chicken, bell peppers, and red onion. Toss until combined and fully coated.

2. Lay 4 large sheets of heavy duty foil on a flat surface. Pour even amounts of prepared ingredients onto the center of each sheet. For each sheet, fold all 4 edges and roll at the middle to seal tightly.

3. Place foil packets onto grill on indirect heat. Cook for about 20 to 25 minutes until chicken is thoroughly cooked.

4. Serve.

Grilled Sausage and Asparagus Foil Packets

Ready in just about 30 minutes, this dish is perfect for people who like a bit of a garlicky flavor with their meat and vegetables.

Serves: 4 – Preparation Time: 10 minutes – Cooking Time: 20 minutes

Nutritional facts per serving: calories 381, total fat 35 g, saturated fat 7 g, carbs 12 g, sugar 0 g, fibers 4 g, protein 8 g, sodium 419 mg

Ingredients

1 bundle asparagus, rinsed and ends trimmed

8 sausages links

½ purple onion, sliced and separated into rings

2 tablespoons garlic, minced

Salt and pepper, to taste

Garlic powder, to taste

8 tablespoons oil

1 lemon, quartered

Preparation

1. Light charcoal briquettes in a chimney starter for about 10 minutes or until gray and ashy. Add to the barbecue pit and placed grill .

2. On a flat surface, spread 4 big sheets of aluminum foil. Onto each foil sheet, distribute even amounts of asparagus, sausages, onion, garlic, salt, pepper, garlic powder, and olive oil. Add them in that order and in layers.

3. Fold up the edges of each sheet and seal the edges together tightly at the center, making sure that there is hardly any air left inside the packet.

4. Add foil packs onto grill and cook for about 20 minutes or until asparagus becomes tender and sausages are cooked through.

5. Remove from heat. Open up the packs just before serving. Garnish with a drizzle of freshly squeezed lemon juice.

Hawaiian Chicken Skewers

Fire up the grill and get this tasty Hawaiian-inspired chicken, pineapple, bell pepper, and onion kebab cooking. This one's complete with a delicious sweet sauce.

Serves: 6 – Preparation Time: 20 minutes – Cooking Time: 15 minutes

Nutritional facts per serving: calories 542, total fat 27 g, saturated fat 9 g, carbs 29 g, sugar 22 g, fibers 2 g, protein 43 g, sodium 947 mg

Ingredients

Sauce

1½ cups pineapple juice

1½ tablespoons cornstarch

½ cup brown sugar

2 tablespoons soy sauce

½ teaspoon salt

Skewers

2 pounds chicken breasts, boneless and skinless, cut into bite-sized pieces

1 large pineapple, cut into bite-sized pieces

2 large red bell peppers, cut into bite-sized pieces

1 large onion, cut into bite-sized pieces

12 strips thick cut bacon

12 wooden skewers, soaked in cold water for at least 30 minutes before using

Preparation

<u>To make at home;</u>

1. Add pineapple juice, cornstarch, brown sugar, soy sauce, and salt to a saucepan over high heat. Mix until combined. Bring to a boil and then reduce heat to medium Let simmer for about 2 minutes. Let cool and place in airtight container.

<u>At the campsite;</u>

2. Light charcoal briquettes in a chimney starter for about 10 minutes or until gray and ashy. Add charcoal to the barbecue pit and set the grate on a medium position.

3. While the charcoal is heating, prepare the skewers by alternating chicken, pineapple, bell pepper, and onion. Wrap 1 strip of bacon around each prepared skewer.

4. Place skewers on grill and cook for about 10 to 15 minutes until chicken is cooked through. Make sure to frequently rotate skewers to cook them evenly.

5. In the meantime, heat the sauce on the grill.

6. Remove from heat and transfer to a serving plate. Serve with prepared sauce on the side.

Delicious Ham and Cheese Sandwich

This isn't just your average ham and cheese sandwich. Aside from the two irreplaceable ingredients, this sandwich is also packed with pickles, lettuce, and onions. Yum!

Serves: 4 – Preparation Time: 10 minutes – Cooking Time: 0 minutes

Nutritional facts per serving: calories 440, total fat 13 g, saturated fat 7 g, carbs 58 g, sugar 0 g, fibers 3 g, protein 21 g, sodium 1834 mg

Ingredients

8 thick slices crusty bread

¼ cup pickles (sweet, dill or sour as you like best)

8 Boston bibb lettuce leaves

7 ounces ham, sliced

4 ounces aged cheddar, sliced

12 white pickled onions

Pepper, to taste

Preparation

1. Lay out 4 bread slices onto a plate or board. Layer even amounts of pickles, lettuce, ham, cheddar, and onion onto each slice. Sprinkle pepper on top.

2. Top each slice with remaining bread slices.

3. Serve.

Chili, Chips, and Cheese Bowl

This simple yet appetizing dish takes only 5 ingredients to make and just 5 minutes to prepare.

Serves: 1 – Preparation Time: 4 minutes – Cooking Time: 1 minute

Nutritional facts per serving: calories 401, total fat 23 g, saturated fat 12 g, carbs 31 g, sugar 3 g, fibers 11 g, protein 22 g, sodium 1512 mg

Ingredients

1 cup corn chips

1 cup prepared chili

¼ cup cheddar cheese, grated

2 teaspoons onions, diced

Mustard

Preparation

1. Pour chili into a small pot and heat over camping stove until warm.

2. Add corn chips to a bowl. Layer with warm chili, cheese, and onions.

3. Serve with a drizzle of mustard on top.

Grilled Coconut Shrimp with Zucchini, Squash, and Corn

With yummy vegetables grilled with coconut-and-lime-marinated shrimp, you and your family won't be able to resist this perfect summer camping lunch.

Serves: 4 – Preparation Time: 10 minutes – Cooking Time: 10 minutes

Nutritional facts per serving: calories 398, total fat 19 g, saturated fat 2 g, carbs 29 g, sugar 8 g, fibers 4 g, protein 29 g, sodium 1788 mg

Ingredients

1 small red onion, diced

2 cloves garlic, diced

⅓ cup sweetened coconut, grated

2 tablespoons lime juice

⅓ cup fresh cilantro, diced

¼ cup olive oil

⅓ cup soy sauce

1 pound large raw shrimp, peeled and deveined

1 zucchini, sliced in half and then into ½-inch moons

1 summer squash, sliced in half and then into ½-inch moons

2 cups corn kernels

Preparation

1. At home, prepare the marinade by adding red onion, garlic, coconut, lime juice, cilantro, olive oil, and soy sauce to a food processor. Pulse on high setting until completely mixed and chopped. Pour into a sealable container. Toss in shrimp to coat. Put on lid and keep refrigerated for at least 2 hours or until you leave for your camping trip. Pack in a cooler once travelling.

2. At the campsite, preheat grill to high.

3. Lay out 4 12-inch long sheets of aluminum foil on a flat surface. Distribute even amounts of zucchini, squash, corn, and the marinated shrimp onto the middle of each foil sheet. For each sheet, roll up all the sides and bring them to the center to seal securely. Before sealing, carefully press the sides of the packets to remove any air pockets.

4. Reduce grill to medium heat. Add foil packs to grill. Grill for about 5 minutes. Using an oven mitt, hold the packs by the seals at the top and lightly shake. Close lid again and grill for an additional 2 to 3 minutes.

5. Remove packs from heat and open up foil packs to allow steam to escape.

6. Serve warm.

Cheesy Penne Pasta in a Pot

Whip up this deliciously flavorful pasta in just 15 minutes or less. Everyone's sure to be going to want seconds.

Serves: 6 – Preparation Time: 5 minutes – Cooking Time: 10 minutes

Nutritional facts per serving: calories 911, total fat 39 g, saturated fat 17 g, carbs 98 g, sugar 4 g, fibers 7 g, protein 46x g, sodium 1629 mg

Ingredients

2 tablespoons olive oil

1 pound smoked sausage, thinly sliced

½ medium onion, chopped

2 garlic cloves, finely chopped

1 cup mushrooms, sliced

3 cups penne pasta, uncooked

2 cups chicken stock

1 10-ounce jar roasted peppers, undrained

2 cups jack cheese, shredded

½ cup Parmesan cheese

2 cups fresh spinach

Preparation

1. Light charcoal briquettes in a chimney starter for about 10 minutes or until gray and ashy. Add charcoal to barbecue pit and place grate at a medium position.

2. In a Dutch oven, heat olive oil. Add onions and cook for 1-2 minutes. Add sausage, garlic, and mushrooms. Sauté for 2-5 minutes, until sausage are well browned. Then, stir in pasta, chicken stock, peppers, cheeses, and spinach. Cover with lid. Cook for about 5 to 8 minutes, then remove

lid. Continue to cook while stirring until pasta is cooked to your liking.

3. Turn off heat and transfer mixture into a serving bowl.

4. Serve.

Easy Grilled Reuben Sandwich

Who doesn't love a good Reuben? Prepare this delicious sandwich in just a few simple steps.

Serves: 4 – Preparation Time: 15 minutes – Cooking Time: 30 minutes

Nutritional facts per serving: calories 777, total fat 49 g, saturated fat 17 g, carbs 51 g, sugar 14 g, fibers xx g, protein 37 g, sodium 2637 mg

Ingredients

8 slices rye bread

1 cup Thousand Island dressing

¾ pound corned beef, thinly sliced

½ pound Swiss cheese, thinly sliced

1 cup sauerkraut

Preparation

1. Light charcoal briquettes in a chimney starter for about 10 minutes or until gray and ashy. Add charcoal to the barbecue pit and place grill at the medium position.

2. While charcoal is heating, on a flat surface, lay out 4 12-inch long double sheets of heavy duty foil. Onto each, arrange 2 bread slices one next to the other. Coat top of each with dressing, then distribute even amounts of corned beef, cheese, and sauerkraut. Make a sandwich by placing 1 bread slice on top of its adjacent slice.

3. Wrap each foil sheets over and around each sandwich and seal tightly.

4. Add sandwiches to grill. Cook until bread is nicely toasted and cheese has melted. Make sure to flip sandwiches every 2 minutes for an even cooking.

5. Serve.

Dinner Recipes

Shrimp and Veggies Foil Packets

This healthy seafood foil packet makes a great dinner that's both quick and easy to make.

Serves: 4 – Preparation Time: 10 minutes – Cooking Time: 15 minutes

Nutritional facts per serving: calories 622, total fat 35 g, saturated fat 10 g, carbs 27 g, sugar 5 g, fibers 3 g, protein 49 g, sodium 1375 mg

Ingredients

1½ pounds large shrimp, peeled and deveined

1 12.8-ounce package smoked Andouille sausage, finely sliced

2 ears corn, each cut crosswise into 4-6 pieces

1 pound baby red potatoes, halved

2 tablespoons olive oil

4 teaspoons Cajun seasoning

Salt and pepper, to taste

2 tablespoons fresh parsley leaves, minced

Preparation

1. Preheat camp grill to high heat.

2. Prepare large rectangles of aluminum foil. Then, distribute shrimp, sausage, corn, and potatoes equally onto middle of each rectangles in layers.

3. Fold edges of the foil sheet towards the center. Drizzle olive oil, then sprinkle Cajun seasoning, salt, and pepper to season. Mix ingredients slightly to combine. Bring foil

edges together at the center and seal by rolling them closed.

4. Cook foil packets on hot grill for about 12 to 15 minutes until thoroughly cooked. Turn over after 6-7 minutes.

5. Serve with parsley sprinkled on top.

Grilled Chicken Skewers

This helpful recipe for a tasty Asian-inspired chicken marinade will save your life during your next camping trip.

Serves: 4 – Preparation Time: 5 minutes – Cooking Time: 5 minutes

Nutritional facts per serving: calories 214, total fat 7 g, saturated fat 1 g, carbs 11 g, sugar 6 g, fibers 1 g, protein 28 g, sodium 519 mg

Ingredients

2 tablespoons soy sauce

2 tablespoons brown sugar

1 tablespoon olive oil

1 tablespoon lemon zest

1 large onion, finely chopped

1½ teaspoon ginger, grated

1 teaspoon cumin

1 teaspoon ground coriander

2 chicken breasts, halved and cut into bite-sized chunks

Assorted vegetables

Preparation

1. In a bowl, add soy sauce, brown sugar, olive oil, lemon zest, garlic, onion, ginger, cumin, and coriander. Mix well.

2. Add chicken to a Ziploc bag and pour prepared mixture inside. Seal tightly. Massage bag using your hand to evenly coat chicken. Store in cooler until ready to cook. Let marinate at least 30 minutes.

3. When ready to cook, prepare the barbecue grill with charcoal briquettes.

4. Add chicken pieces to a skewer, alternating with washed vegetables.

5. Grill skewers for about 5 to 6 minutes per side until cooked.

6. Serve.

Delicious Dutch Oven Pepperoni Pizza

Who says you can't make a full-sized pepperoni pizza in the wilderness? Whip this easy coal-baked dish in just 35 minutes.

Serves: 4 – Preparation Time: 20 minutes – Cooking Time: 15 minutes

Nutritional facts per serving: calories 449, total fat 24 g, saturated fat 10 g, carbs 44 g, sugar 6 g, fibers 3 g, protein 16 g, sodium 1694 mg

Ingredients

1 tablespoon vegetable oil

1 12-inch tube pizza dough crust

1 small can tomato sauce

Garlic powder, to taste

Salt, to taste

Pepper, to taste

1 large onion, sliced

15 to 20 pepperoni slices

½ cup mozzarella cheese, grated

¼ cup cheddar cheese, shredded

Preparation

1. Heat coals for cooking.

2. Drizzle vegetable oil in a Dutch oven and move it around to spread onto the entire bottom and sides of the vessel.

3. Roll out pizza dough and cut in half. Line bottom of Dutch oven with one half of pizza dough, then line the sides with the other half.

4. Spoon tomato sauce onto dough and spread to coat entire surface. Scatter garlic powder, salt, and pepper. Evenly distribute onion and pepperoni on top.

73

5. Next, position Dutch oven a ring of hot coals. Cover, then put a few hot coals on the Dutch oven's lid. Cook for about 10 minutes. Remove lid, then scatter mozzarella and cheddar cheese onto hot pizza. Return lid and add more hot coals to melt the cheese quicker.

6. Pizza is ready to serve once cheese has melted.

Campfire Herbs-and-Lemon Salmon Fillets

This 15-minute gourmet-like dish is quick, easy to make, and super delicious. The secret? Aluminum foil.

Serves: 4 – Preparation Time: 5 minutes – Cooking Time: 10 minutes

Nutritional facts per serving: calories 302, total fat 14 g, saturated fat 8 g, carbs 9 g, sugar 0 g, fibers 1 g, protein 33 g, sodium 655 mg

Ingredients

4 salmon fillets

Salt and pepper, to taste

4 tablespoons Dijon mustard

8 lemon slices

4 sprigs tarragon

4 sprigs dill

1 shallot, sliced

4 tablespoons butter

2 cloves garlic, finely chopped

Olive Oil

Preparation

1. Generously sprinkle salmon fillets with salt and pepper. Then, coat 1 tablespoon Dijon mustard onto the tops of each fillet followed by 2 lemon slices, a sprig of tarragon and dill, shallot slices, 1 tablespoon butter, and garlic. Drizzle a generous amount of olive oil on top.

2. Transfer each fillet onto individual sheets of aluminum foil. Wrap by folding the edges to the center. Roll the edges together to securely close.

3. Cook foil wraps by placing them directly onto campfire coals for about 6 to 8 minutes until cooked.

4. Serve.

Camping Beef and Vegetables Stew

This hearty stew is best to be shared and enjoyed with friends and family during one of those colder camping nights.

Serves: 6 – Preparation Time: 15 minutes – Cooking Time: 2 hours 30 minutes

Nutritional facts per serving: calories 442, total fat 21 g, saturated fat 7 g, carbs 26 g, sugar 0 g, fibers 6 g, protein 38 g, sodium 582 mg

Ingredients

6 cloves garlic, finely chopped

2 tablespoons fresh rosemary leaves, coarsely chopped

2 tablespoons olive oil

1 teaspoon kosher salt, plus more to season

½ teaspoon pepper, plus more to season

2 pounds beef chuck roast, boneless

1 pint cherry tomatoes, stems removed

2 ears corn, cleaned and cut into thirds

1 onion, cut into 6 wedges

½ pound green beans, halved and ends trimmed

6 baby zucchini, ends trimmed

¾ pound small potatoes

2 tablespoons butter

3 cups chicken broth, divided

Preparation

1. Prepare seasoned beef at home by mixing garlic, rosemary, oil, 1 teaspoon salt, and ½ teaspoon pepper in a small bowl. Add beef into a Ziploc bag and pour marinade mixture inside. Seal tightly. Massage bag with your hand to evenly coat beef. Store in refrigerator or freezer until camping trip, or at most 2 days.

2. Next, also at home, add tomatoes, corn, and onion in a separate Ziploc bag. Add green beans and zucchini in a third bag. Store both bags in refrigerator or freezer until camping trip, or at most 2 days.

3. When ready to serve, prepare fire by heating up coals in a chimney starter or campfire.

4. Once coals are hot, form a circle and position a Dutch oven on top. Melt butter in Dutch oven. Then, add beef and cook for about 10 minutes until dark-colored on one side. Flip meat, then pour 2 cups broth. Put on lid, and place a few hot coals on top. Cook for 30 minutes. Add a few more coals on lid as needed, then continue cooking for another 30 minutes.

5. Flip meat again, then add another 1 cup broth. Mix in prepared vegetables and potatoes. Return lid and cook for 1 more hour. Flip meat and corn once more. Stir in beans and zucchini. Place lid back on Dutch oven and cook for 15 to 30 minutes until meat becomes very soft. Sprinkle salt and pepper to taste to adjust seasoning.

6. Serve.

Dutch Oven Mac and Cheese

Cooked using 3 different types of cheeses, this appetizing yet simple macaroni and cheese dish is cooked in a Dutch oven over hot coals.

Serves: 4 – Preparation Time: 10 minutes – Cooking Time: 15 minutes

Nutritional facts per serving: calories 497, total fat 31 g, saturated fat 19 g, carbs 32 g, sugar 3 g, fibers 1 g, protein 24 g, sodium 537 mg

Ingredients

2 cups elbow macaroni

Water for boiling

3 tablespoons butter

½ cup milk

2 tablespoons flour

Salt and pepper, to taste

1 cup gruyere cheese, grated

½ cup sharp cheddar cheese, grated

½ cup Gouda cheese, grated

½ cup bread crumbs

Preparation

1. Light charcoal briquettes until gray and ashy in the barbecue. and place a grill grate on top. Then, place Dutch oven on top and cook pasta following package instructions. Drain pasta and set aside to cool.

2. Return pan over hot coals. Add butter. Once melted, stir in milk. Drop flour, 1 tablespoon at a time, stirring continuously, until mixture becomes thick. Season with salt and pepper.

3. Gently stir in gruyere, cheddar, and Gouda cheese into mixture. Retain some cheese for topping.

4. Toss in cooked macaroni and mix well to coat with cheese sauce. Place lid on Dutch oven and cook for about 5 minutes until thoroughly heated.

5. Remove lid and sprinkle remaining cheese and bread crumbs. Return lid. Cook for another 5 minutes.

6. Serve.

Grilled Stuffed Potato

These baked potatoes are sliced and generously stuffed with ham, cheese, and bacon, then grilled while inside foil packets for a gooey, crispy, and hot potato dinner.

Serves: 2 – Preparation Time: 5 minutes – Cooking Time: 25 minutes

Nutritional facts per serving: calories 756, total fat 35 g, saturated fat 18 g, carbs 67 g, sugar 4 g, fibers 7 g, protein 44 g, sodium 2376 mg

Ingredients

2 large potatoes, baked

6 slices American cheese, cut in half

4 slices bacon, cooked and cut into 3 pieces

6 slices ham, cut in half

Non-stick cooking spray

Sour cream

Scallions, chopped

Salt and pepper to taste

Preparation

1. Cut baked potatoes horizontally into 6 thick slices. Salt and pepper potatoes to taste.

2. Evenly distribute cheese, bacon, and ham in between each slice.

3. Coat non-stick cooking spray onto inner side of a 2-layer sheet of aluminum foil. Then, transfer stuffed potato onto foil. Fold edges towards the center to wrap. Roll edges together to close packet securely. Do the same for the 2nd potato.

4. Cook on hot camp grill or camp fire for about 20 minutes or until ingredients have melted together and potato is heated through.

5. Open up packet and serve with sour cream and scallions on top.

Foil Packet Stuffed Onions

These gourmet stuffed onions are savory with a bit of spiciness. Coal-cooked to perfection, this dish makes a wonderful dinner for the family.

Serves: 4 – Preparation Time: 10 minutes – Cooking Time: 30 minutes

Nutritional facts per serving: calories 667, total fat 18 g, saturated fat 7 g, carbs 79 g, sugar 3 g, fibers 15 g, protein 48 g, sodium 1857 mg

Ingredients

4 extra-large sweet onions

1 pound pork sirloin, finely sliced and cubed

½ teaspoon ground cumin

1 cup boxed cornbread stuffing mix

2 tablespoons mild green chili powder

3 large poblano chilies, roasted, peeled and seeded

1 15½-ounce can hominy, drained

¼ cup sweet red pepper, diced

½ cup Parmesan cheese, grated

2 teaspoons coarse kosher salt

Black pepper, to taste

Cilantro

Avocado

Preparation

1. Cut off about ¼ of the onion from the top. Then, cut off the bottom of the onion so that it can stand upright without rolling. Peel onions. Cut an 'X' at the middle of the onion. Then, scoop out the insides of onions until you only have a ½-inch thick wall. Take ¼ cup onion you took out from the inside and chop them. Discard remaining onion.

2. In a bowl, add chopped onion, pork, cumin, stuffing mix, chili powder, poblano chilies, hominy, red pepper, cheese, salt, and pepper. Mix well until blended. Spoon out mixture and transfer to the inside of hollow onions until each onion is filled. Place onions onto sheets of thick foil, then wrap. Seal edges by rolling them together in the center.

3. Cook on hot coals with a few coals resting on top of each foil packet. Allow to cook for about 30 minutes. Remove from heat. Check one packet to see if onion is soft and cooked through. If not, reseal and continue cooking for a few more minutes.

4. Open foil packets and top with cilantro and avocado before serving.

25-Minute Colorful Seafood and Bacon Dinner

Sea scallops paired with bacon, all cooked together in an assortment of hearty vegetables, makes this a colorful and flavorful dinner that everyone will enjoy.

Serves: 4 – Preparation Time: 10 minutes – Cooking Time: 15 minutes

Nutritional facts per serving: calories 361, total fat 7 g, saturated fat 1 g, carbs 19 g, sugar 12 g, fibers 3 g, protein 45 g, sodium 1693 mg

Ingredients

5 slices thick cut bacon

1⅓ pounds fresh sea scallops

2 tablespoons blackening seasoning

3 scallions, diced

⅔ cup red bell pepper, diced

3 ears fresh sweet corn, kernels cut from the cob

3 cloves garlic, diced

½ cup white wine

2 medium ripe tomatoes, diced

½ cup fresh basil plus extra for garnish, diced

3 tablespoons fresh lime juice

Salt and pepper to taste

Preparation

1. Cook bacon in a cast iron pan over hot coals until crispy. Drain and set aside.

2. Return pan to heat and add sea scallops and blackening seasoning. Cook for about 2 minutes on each side. They should be heated through but not cooked. Remove from pan and set aside.

3. Stir fry scallions, red pepper, and corn in same pan for about 4 minutes. Stir in garlic and cook for 1 more minute. Then, pour in wine to soften any substances hardened on the bottom. Scrape them into the mixture and cook for about 2 minutes.

4. Stir in tomato, basil, lime juice, salt, and pepper into pan. Let simmer for 2 minutes, then mix in scallops. Simmer for another 5 minutes.

5. Serve in bowls topped with crumbled bacon and basil.

Coal-Cooked Sausage and Herbs Pizza

This meaty pizza is cooked right on the grate over some hot coals.

Serves: 16 – Preparation Time: 30 minutes – Cooking Time: 30 minutes

Nutritional facts per serving: calories 170, total fat 13 g, saturated fat 6 g, carbs 4 g, sugar 1 g, fibers 1 g, protein 8 g, sodium 429 mg

Ingredients

1 pound mild Italian ground sausages

1 medium bulb fennel, cored and sliced

½ large onion, sliced

Salt and pepper, to taste

Olive oil

1 bag prepared pizza dough

Pizza sauce

8 ounces fresh mozzarella cheese, sliced

¼ cup pine nuts

Fennel fronds, chopped

Preparation

1. Light coals until gray and ashy. Then, place cast iron pan onto a grated grill over hot coals. Heat oil in pan and add ground sausages. Break apart sausage while cooking so that you'll have browned bite-sized pieces once done. Remove from pan and set aside.

2. Heat more oil in pan, then add fennel and onion. Sprinkle salt and pepper to season. Stir fry until lightly brown and tender. Remove from pan and set aside. Remove grill and allow to cool.

3. Once cool, clean grill by wiping it using a clean, wet piece of cloth. You'll know it's clean once little to no soot is seen on the cloth. Let dry then wipe with olive oil to grease. Return above hot coals. The temperature is perfect for cooking once the heat from coals is hot enough that you can keep your hand above them at the same level of the grill for 10 seconds, no more and no less.

4. Divide dough into two equal halves. Then, roll them out to form 10-inch pizza crusts. Place dough onto hot grill and cook for about 5 minutes until crisp and grill lines form on the back. Turn dough over.

5. Cover pizza with just enough sauce to coat, then add half of the mozzarella, fennel, onions, sausage, and pine nuts equally over the dough. The other half of the ingredients will be for the 2nd pizza. Cover pizza using a metal lid or aluminum foil to melt the cheese and thoroughly heat toppings. Cook for about 5 minutes until cheese is melted. Remove from heat and grill. Repeat the process with 2nd pizza.

6. Slice and serve with remaining fennel fronds sprinkled on top.

Grilled Lamb, Onion, and Pepper Skewers with Pesto Sauce

Don't be fooled by this kebab's gourmet taste and appearance because this is dish is as easy as it is delicious. Pesto sauce should be prepared at home.

Serves: 6 – Preparation Time: 1 minute – Cooking Time: 10 minutes

Nutritional facts per serving: calories 517, total fat 39 g, saturated fat 10 g, carbs 7 g, sugar 2 g, fibers 2 g, protein 34 g, sodium 515 mg

Ingredients

1 cup fresh mint leaves

½ cup fresh cilantro leaves

2 tablespoons pine nuts

2 tablespoons Parmesan cheese, shredded

1 tablespoon fresh lemon juice

1 medium clove garlic, peeled

2½ teaspoons coarse kosher salt, divided

½ cup + 1 tablespoon extra-virgin olive oil, plus more for brushing

4 large garlic cloves, finely chopped

1½ teaspoons ground coriander seeds

2 pounds lamb leg, trimmed, boneless, and chopped into 1¼-inch cubes

2 large red bell peppers, cut into 1-inch squares

1 large red onion, cut into 1-inch squares

Preparation

<u>At home preparation:</u>

1. Prepare pesto ahead of time. In a food processor, make pesto sauce by adding mint, cilantro, pine nuts, Parmesan cheese, lemon juice, 1 clove garlic, and ½ teaspoon salt. Process until ingredients form a lumpy mixture. Then, while still processing, slowly add ½ cup oil until mixture is smooth. Remove from processor container and transfer to container. Sprinkle salt and pepper, to taste. Cover with lid and keep cool until ready to use.

<u>At campsite:</u>

2. For the kebabs, combine 1 tablespoon oil, finely chopped garlic, 2 teaspoons salt, and coriander in a bowl. Toss in lamb and coat evenly. Cover bowl, and place inside cooler for 2 to 4 hours.

3. When ready to cook, preheat grill to medium-high heat. Add lamb pieces, peppers, and onions to skewers. Alternate each ingredient with one another as you thread them through the skewers. Then, arrange skewers onto baking sheet. Coat with oil using a brush. Season with pepper. Place onto hot grill and cook for about 7 to 9 minutes, rotating halfway through. This will result to medium-rare doneness.

4. Transfer cooked skewers to a serving plate. Lightly coat each piece with prepared pesto sauce from earlier. Serve with leftover pesto sauce on the side.

Easy Toasted Crescent Roll Hot Dog

This simple dish is really easy to make—and it's fun, too! Make the kids help prepare this tasty dish for a light outdoor dinner with the family.

Serves: 8 – Preparation Time: 5 minutes – Cooking Time: 10 minutes

Nutritional facts per serving: calories 301, total fat 23 g, saturated fat 9 g, carbs 16 g, sugar 3 g, fibers 0 g, protein 7 g, sodium 1016 mg

Ingredients

1 tube refrigerated crescent rolls

8 hot dogs

Mustard

Ketchup

Preparation

1. Roll out crescent roll dough onto a flat surface. Divide into 8 equal triangles.

2. Starting at one edge, roll dough to wrap hot dog. The entire hot dog does not need to be wrapped, ends may be left exposed. Lightly press the end of the dough onto the overlapping dough to secure.

3. Pierce skewer into hot dog and cook over campfire like you would marshmallows. It's best to keep hot dogs slightly away from direct fire but cook it in an area that is still quite hot. This will let the dogs cook evenly.

4. Once cooked and well toasted, serve right away with mustard and ketchup drizzled on top or on the side.

Camping Sausage and Potato Hash

This is an amazing dish to prepare and enjoy after a long day of having fun in the outdoors.

Serves: 6 – Preparation Time: 15 minutes – Cooking Time: 40 minutes

Nutritional facts per serving: calories 493, total fat 26 g, saturated fat 7 g, carbs 51 g, sugar 9 g, fibers 8 g, protein 15 g, sodium 1008 mg

Ingredients

2 tablespoons canola oil

1 large onion, diced

2 cloves garlic, finely chopped

2 pounds potatoes, peeled and cubed

1 pound Polish sausage, halved and sliced

1 4-ounce can green chilies, chopped

1 15¼-ounce can whole kernel corn, drained

Preparation

1. Heat oil in a large cast iron pan over medium heat. Once hot, add onion and sauté until almost soft. Then, stir in garlic and sauté for 1 minute. Mix in potatoes and cook for about 20 minutes while stirring ingredients occasionally.

2. Then, toss in sausage. Stir fry for an additional 10 minutes or until soft and meat and potatoes are browned. Mix in chilies and corn.

3. Serve.

Grilled Hot Dog and Potato Foil Packets

Too tired after a full day of outdoor activities? Prepare this minimal-effort dish that is packed with maximum delicious flavor.

Serves: 4 – Preparation Time: 5 minutes – Cooking Time: 15 minutes

Nutritional facts per serving: calories 306, total fat 16 g, saturated fat 7 g, carbs 30 g, sugar 7 g, fibers 3 g, protein 10 g, sodium 837 mg

Ingredients

20 red potato wedges

4 hot dogs

1 small onion, cut into wedges

¼ cup cheddar cheese, grated

½ cup barbecue sauce

Preparation

1. Distribute potatoes among 4 large sheets of thick aluminum foil. Then, layer hot dog, onion, and cheese on top of potatoes. Add a drizzle of barbecue sauce on top. Wrap edges of foil over ingredients and roll together at the center to seal securely.

2. Place on grill and cook for about 10 to 15 minutes over medium heat. Remove from grill and open foil.

3. Allow to cool for a bit before serving.

Mexican-inspired Chicken and Beans Foil Packs

This easy-to-make 35-minute dinner is a delicious Mexican-inspired dish with ingredients such as chicken, beans, corn, tomatoes, and cheese. Yum!

Serves: 4 – Preparation Time: 10 minutes – Cooking Time: 25 minutes

Nutritional facts per serving: calories 555, total fat 13 g, saturated fat 5 g, carbs 41 g, sugar 2 g, fibers 13 g, protein 67 g, sodium 510 mg

Ingredients

1 15-ounce can navy beans, drained and rinsed

1 10-ounce can diced tomatoes

1 can corn kernels

1 tablespoon Mexican spice blend

4 chicken breasts, boneless and skinless, cut into strips

½ cup Mexican cheese blend, grated

Scallions, chopped

Preparation

1. Lay out 4 12-inch long sheets of aluminum foil onto a flat surface.

2. In a bowl, add beans, tomatoes, corn, spice blend, and chicken. Mix until well combined. Then, divide mixture evenly among the 4 foil sheets, placing each onto the center. Roll up the edges of the sheets and fold at the top to secure tightly.

3. Place a grill grate over your campfire and arrange foil packs onto grate. Grill for about 20 to 25 minutes until chicken is cooked through. Remove from heat.

4. Open up packets and garnish with cheese and scallions.

5. Serve.

BBQ Chicken and Vegetable Foil Packs

Tender chicken and an assortment of hearty vegetables all foil-wrapped and cooked to perfection over the grill—this dish makes a perfect meal to end a great day at camp.

Serves: 4 – Preparation Time: 10 minutes – Cooking Time: 25 minutes

Nutritional facts per serving: calories 248, total fat 11 g, saturated fat 2 g, carbs 10 g, sugar 3 g, fibers 2 g, protein 28 g, sodium 396 mg

Ingredients

4 4-ounce chicken breasts, boneless and skinless

Salt and pepper to taste

½ cup barbecue sauce

1 zucchini, thinly sliced

1 red bell pepper, julienned

8 asparagus spears

Extra-virgin olive oil

Preparation

1. Set grill to medium-high heat.

2. Place each chicken breast onto a double layer of aluminum foil. Sprinkle salt and pepper, to taste.

3. Next, spread about 1 to 2 tablespoons barbecue sauce onto each chicken breast.

4. Then, distribute equal amounts zucchini, bell peppers, and asparagus onto the foil surrounding each chicken breast. Sprinkle salt and pepper, to taste. Top ingredients with a drizzle of olive oil.

5. Wrap ingredients in aluminum foil by folding edges towards the center and rolling them together to seal completely.

6. Place onto hot grill and cook for about 10 to 12 minutes. Flip foil packs and cook other side for another 10 to 13 minutes. Chicken is fully cooked once meat thermometer registers 165 °F. Remove from grill.

7. Open foil packets and serve.

30-minute Camping Grilled Steak

This classic grilled steak is cooked to perfection using an uncommon yet simple grilling method. This one's definitely a must-try.

Serves: 2 – Preparation Time: 10 minutes – Cooking Time: 20 minutes

Nutritional facts per serving: calories 937, total fat 39 g, saturated fat 16 g, carbs 1 g, sugar 0 g, fibers 0 g, protein 133 g, sodium 1921 mg

Ingredients

1 2-pound 2-inch-thick bone-in rib eye steak

2 teaspoons kosher salt

1 teaspoon black peppercorns, roughly cracked

Vegetable oil, for brushing

Coarse sea salt, to taste

Preparation

1. Using a paper towel, dab steak to make it dry then put on top of a wire rack. Sprinkle with ½ teaspoon salt on each side. Set aside at room temperature for about 1 hour or more.

2. Dab steak again using a paper towel. Sprinkle another ½ teaspoon salt on each side to season a second time. Then, sprinkle ½ teaspoon peppercorns on each side. Rub black peppercorns onto steak to make them stick.

3. Prepare your grill by creating 2 zones for cooking, medium-high and medium-low. Coat grill grate with oil using a brush. Add steak onto the medium-high zone and grill for about 3 to 4 minutes per side, turning once. Transfer steak to the medium-low zone and grill for another 3 to 4 minutes per side, turning once.

4. Next, use a pair of tongs to cook the steak on its sides. Grill sides for about 1 to 2 minutes until fat is rendered.

5. The steak should cook for a total of 14 to 18 minutes and should reach the internal temperature of 120 °F for rare doneness, while it could rise up to 125 °F or higher, while resting, for medium-rare.

6. Remove from heat then place onto a cutting board. Allow steak to rest for about 10 minutes. Slice against the grain. Sprinkle with coarse sea salt to season.

7. Serve.

Rosemary and Sage Trout Wrapped in Bacon

Thinking about going fishing for your next camping trip? This is an excellent dish to cook with freshly caught trout and a few other delicious ingredients.

Serves: 6 – Preparation Time: 10 minutes – Cooking Time: 30 minutes

Nutritional facts per serving: calories 327, total fat 15 g, saturated fat 5 g, carbs 3 g, sugar 0 g, fibers 1 g, protein 42 g, sodium 462 mg

Ingredients

2 1-pound trout, gutted, scaled, and butterflied

Salt and pepper, to taste

Garlic powder, to taste

6 sprigs fresh rosemary

6 sprigs fresh sage

1 onion, finely sliced

12 ounces thin-cut bacon

Preparation

1. Rinse trout and dab with a paper towel to dry. Season insides with salt, pepper, and garlic powder. Then, add 3 sprigs rosemary, 3 sprigs rosemary, and ½ of the onion. Close the trout. Wrap a strip of bacon around the trout, completely coating it. If one strip is not enough, use another and continue wrapping around trout. Secure the beginning of 2nd strip under the end of the 1st one, then tuck the end of the 2nd strip under itself. Keep the fish head in place by wrapping it with bacon as well. Repeat with 2nd trout.

2. Place a grill grate over some hot coals, then arrange the trout onto the grill grate. Cook for about 10 to 15 minutes on each side, turning once. The trout are done once the

bacon becomes crisp all over and the trout is soft enough to easily pierce.

3. Remove from heat and transfer to a plate.

4. Serve.

Delicious 30-minute Grilled Campfire Hamburgers

Crispy bacon, melted cheddar cheese, caramelized onions, savory beef patties, and a delicious chipotle-infused sauce all sandwiched in between two buttered, toasted buns.

Serves: 4 – Preparation Time: 10 minutes – Cooking Time: 20 minutes

Nutritional facts per serving: calories 1054, total fat 78 g, saturated fat 24 g, carbs 38 g, sugar 8 g, fibers 3 g, protein 49 g, sodium 3323 mg

Ingredients

1 cup mayonnaise

1 cup barbecue sauce

1 teaspoon dried chipotle powder

1 pound thin-cut bacon

2 yellow onions, sliced

4 hamburger patties

4 slices cheddar cheese

4 hamburger buns, split horizontally

2 tablespoons butter, softened

Preparation

<u>Preparation at home</u>

1. At home, prepare the sauce by combining mayonnaise, barbecue sauce, and chipotle powder in a bowl. Mix well and transfer to a sealable container. Store inside the refrigerator until you're ready to leave for your camping trip, then transfer to a cooler when travelling.

<u>At the campsite,</u>

2. Light charcoal briquettes in a chimney starter for about 10 minutes or until gray and ashy. Add charcoal in barbecue pit and place grill to the medium position.

3. Cook bacon in a large pan over a camping stove. Keep bacon grease in the pan. Once crispy, transfer to a plate and set aside.

4. Return pan to heat and add onion. Sauté until lightly brown and tender, about 2 minutes. Remove from pan and set aside.

5. Place hamburger patties onto grill and cook for 3 minutes and flip. Continue grilling for another 4-8 minutes until desired doneness. In the last minute or so, position cheese on top of each patties and let melt. Remove burgers. Set aside.

6. Coat the insides of the hamburger buns with butter and place on grill until nicely toasted. Remove from heat and transfer to a plate.

7. To assemble the burgers, spread the buttered sides of the hamburger buns with prepared sauce from earlier. Place cooked patties on top, followed by the cooked bacon and onions. Top with second bun.

8. Serve.

Salsa Verde Baked Salmon in Foil

Full of spices and flavors, this recipe will make Mexican food lovers very happy!

Serves: 4 – Preparation Time: 10 minutes – Cooking Time: 15 minutes

Nutritional facts per serving: calories 623, total fat 30 g, saturated fat 5 g, carbs 22 g, sugar 4 g, fibers 5 g, protein 67 g, sodium 264 mg

Ingredients

Salsa

1 small bunch flat leaf parsley

10 cloves fresh garlic, crushed

1 teaspoon chili flakes, crushed

1 pint cherry tomatoes, halved

⅓ cup extra-virgin olive oil

Other ingredients

Water, for boiling

1¼ pounds fresh green beans, ends trimmed

2 teaspoons olive oil

Salt and pepper, to taste

1 large lemon, quartered

Preparation

1. Light charcoal briquettes in a chimney starter for about 10 minutes or until gray and ashy. Add charcoal in barbecue pit and place grill to the medium position.

2. In a bowl, prepare salsa by adding parsley, garlic, chili flakes, tomatoes, and extra-virgin olive oil. Mix well until combined. Set aside.

3. Fill up a medium pot with water and bring to a boil over the grill or a camping stove. Add green beans once water is boiling. Cook for about 3 minutes. Drain, then add to a separate bowl. Pour 2 teaspoons olive oil into the bowl and sprinkle salt and pepper.

4. Lay out 4 14-inch long sheets of aluminum foil onto a flat surface. Add ¼ boiled green beans to the center of each sheet followed by salmon and top with ¼ tomato salsa.

5. Fold the edges of the foil packs towards the center and roll them together to seal. Make sure to leave some space inside the packs to let the air circulate.

6. Arrange foil packs onto grill and cook for about 10 to 15 minutes.

7. Serve each with a drizzle of juice from 1 lemon quarter.

Dutch Oven Chicken and Cheese

Cooked with chicken, bacon, cheese, potatoes, carrots, onions, and Sprite, this super appetizing one-pot dish could a feed your entire family and the next.

Serves: 20 – Preparation Time: 30 minutes – Cooking Time: 45 minutes

Nutritional facts per serving: calories 222, total fat 7 g, saturated fat 4 g, carbs 31 g, sugar 6 g, fibers 4 g, protein 10 g, sodium 284 mg

Ingredients

1 pound bacon

1 cup flour

1 tablespoon seasoning salt

2 pounds boneless and skinless chicken, cut into bite-sized pieces

3 large onions, quartered

5 pounds red potatoes, cut into 2-inch cubes

2 pounds carrots, cut into thirds

1 can Sprite

2 cups cheddar cheese, grated

Preparation

1. Add bacon to a Dutch oven and cook on camping stove. Once bacon turns crispy, remove from Dutch oven and transfer to a plate. Leave bacon grease inside the vessel.

2. In a bowl, add flour and seasoning salt. Mix well until combined, then toss in chicken to coat evenly.

3. Using the same Dutch oven with the bacon grease inside, add coated chicken and cook until nicely browned. Remove chicken from vessel and transfer to the same plate as the bacon.

4. Transfer Dutch oven to a single, flat layer of hot coals. Then, add onions, potatoes, carrots, chicken, bacon, and sprite in layers and in that order. Next, place the lid on top and arrange more hot coals over the lid.

5. Let cook for 45 minutes. Remove lid and add cheese. Return lid and let cook for an additional 10 minutes or until cheese is melted.

6. Serve.

Marinated Grilled Lamb and Beef

This grilled meat platter is perfect if you're searching for something a little more gourmet to prepare at camp, but still easy to make. This one's sure to wow your guests.

Serves: 8 – Preparation Time: 15 minutes – Cooking Time: 10 minutes

Nutritional facts per serving: calories 510, total fat 34 g, saturated fat 12 g, carbs 9 g, sugar 8 g, fibers 1 g, protein 40 g, sodium 445 mg

Ingredients

⅓ cup balsamic vinegar, divided

1 tablespoon brown sugar

1 tablespoon fresh rosemary, diced

1 garlic clove, crushed

Salt and pepper, to taste

8 lamb chops, ¾-inch thick

8 small beef rump steaks, about ¾-inch thick

¼ cup sun-dried tomato pesto

8 slices pancetta

½ cup tomato chutney

Preparation

<u>At home preparation:</u>
1. At home, prepare marinated lamb chops by adding ¼ cup balsamic vinegar, brown sugar, rosemary, garlic, salt, and pepper to a bowl. Place lamb chops into bowl and flip to soak in marinade. Cover bowl and store in refrigerator for at most 4 hours. Store in a cooler once traveling

<u>At the campsite:</u>
2. Light charcoal briquettes in a chimney starter for about 10 minutes or until gray and ashy. Add charcoal in barbecue pit and place grill to the medium position.
3. Place steaks onto a flat surface and rub all sides with pesto. Sprinkle salt and pepper to season.
4. Prepare lamb chops by draining and discarding marinade from its container.
5. Add lamb and beef onto grill and cook for 3 to 4 minutes per side for medium-rare. You make cook them for a shorter or longer time depending on your preferred doneness.
6. Remove from heat. Arrange them on a plate and loosely cover them with a sheet of aluminum foil. Set aside for about 5 minutes to rest.
7. Add pancetta to grill and cook for about 1 minutes per side. Remove from heat.
8. Mix chutney and remaining vinegar in a small bowl.
9. Arrange lamb chops, beef steaks, and pancetta on a platter. Serve with chutney mixture.

Grilled Chicken with Mozzarella, Tomato, and Balsamic Vinegar

This is a delicious and healthy dish that takes only 30 minutes to make.

Serves: 6 – Preparation Time: 5 minutes – Cooking Time: 25 minutes

Nutritional facts per serving: calories 398, total fat 15 g, saturated fat 7 g, carbs 3 g, sugar 0 g, fibers 0 g, protein 60 g, sodium 323 mg

Ingredients

6 chicken breasts, boneless and skinless

Salt and pepper

1 teaspoon garlic powder

¼ cup balsamic vinegar

1 tablespoon butter

6 slices mozzarella cheese

6 slices tomato

6 large basil leaves

Preparation

1. Light charcoal briquettes in a chimney starter for about 10 minutes or until gray and ashy. Add charcoal in barbecue pit and place grill to the medium position.

2. Season chicken with salt, pepper, and garlic powder. Let rest for 5 minutes.

3. Place chicken on grill and cook for 3 minutes and flip. Continue cooking until cooked though, about 4-6 minutes. Remove from heat and set aside.

4. Add balsamic vinegar to a pan and cook on a camping stove or grill until greatly reduced. Stir in butter until melted and incorporated. Remove from heat and reserve for later.

5. Layer mozzarella, basil, and tomato on top of chicken. Place on grill for an additional 1-2 minutes, until cheese start melting and chicken is warmed.

6. To serve, lightly pour balsamic reduction on top.

Grilled Chicken Mushroom Soup Foil Packs

This is an easy warm and hearty chicken stew that's great for one of those colder nights out at camp.

Serves: 4 – Preparation Time: 30 minutes – Cooking Time: 40 minutes

Nutritional facts per serving: calories 924, total fat 23 g, saturated fat 6 g, carbs 43 g, sugar 4 g, fibers 7 g, protein 128 g, sodium 1071 mg

Ingredients

1 3½-pound whole chicken, cut into pieces

1 teaspoon salt

½ teaspoon pepper

1 teaspoon paprika

3 medium potatoes, peeled and sliced

1 cup carrots, finely sliced

1 medium green pepper, sliced

1 10¾-ounce can condensed cream of mushroom soup

¼ cup water

Preparation

1. Light charcoal briquettes in a chimney starter for about 10 minutes or until gray and ashy. Add charcoal in barbecue pit and place grill to the medium position.

2. Season chicken with salt, pepper, and paprika. Place chicken onto grill and brown for 3 minutes and then flip over. Continue grilling for another 3 minutes, or until chicken is well browned.

3. Lay out 2 24-inch long double-layered sheets of heavy duty aluminum foil. Once chicken is cooked through, transfer to the foil sheets. Place half of the chicken pieces per foil sheet.

4. Evenly distribute potatoes, carrots, and green pepper among foil sheets. Fold sides up of each foil sheet to create a box shape, then divide mushroom soup, water, salt, and pepper evenly among the foil packs.

5. For each foil pack, roll up the edges to the center and fold to seal tightly to avoid any leakages.

6. Place foil packs onto grill and close lid. Grill for about 20 to 25 minutes per side, turning once.

7. Use oven mitts to carefully open foil packs. Let the steam escape.

8. Serve hot.

Grilled Teriyaki Chicken Foil Packs

This delicious dish is a combination of tasty grilled chicken bits, pineapple, bell peppers, and onion, all swimming in a delicious Asian-inspired teriyaki and sesame sauce.

Serves: 4 – Preparation Time: 10 minutes – Cooking Time: 20 minutes

Nutritional facts per serving: calories 602, total fat 19 g, saturated fat 4 g, carbs 47 g, sugar 39 g, fibers 2 g, protein 60 g, sodium 608 mg

Ingredients

1 cup teriyaki sauce

1 cup toasted sesame dressing

4 chicken breasts, boneless and skinless, chopped into 1½-inch pieces

1 red bell pepper, diced

1 green bell pepper, diced

1 small onion, diced

1½ cups pineapple chunks

Preparation

1. Light charcoal briquettes in a chimney starter for about 10 minutes or until gray and ashy. Add charcoal in barbecue pit and place grill to the medium position.

2. Add teriyaki sauce and sesame dressing to a large bowl. Add chicken and mix until combined.

3. On a flat surface, lay out 4 24-inch long double layered sheets of heavy duty foil. Divide chicken mixture among the 4 sheets, placing each on the center.

4. Roll up the edges of the sheets and fold at the center to seal tightly and securely.

5. Place foil packs onto the grill and cook until chicken is cooked thoroughly, about 20-25 minutes.

6. Remove from heat and open up one foil packet. Check doneness. If not ready, fold back tightly and continue cooking for a few more minutes.

7. When ready, carefully unfold the packets and let steam out.

8. To serve, sprinkle cilantro and sesame seeds.

Asian-inspired Beef and Vegetables on Sticks

Cut into bite-sized pieces and cooked on the grill with skewers, this is a tasty dish that incorporates a delicious Asian flavor to the beef.

Serves: 4 – Preparation Time: 10 minutes – Cooking Time: 10 minutes

Nutritional facts per serving: calories 224, total fat 12 g, saturated fat 2 g, carbs 8 g, sugar 6 g, fibers 2 g, protein 21 g, sodium 365 mg

Ingredients

Marinade and steak

2 tablespoons oyster sauce

1 tablespoon soy sauce

2 tablespoons olive oil, divided

2 teaspoon garlic, diced

1 teaspoon sesame oil

1 pound strip loin steak, fat trimmed and cut into 1-inch chunks

Other ingredients

1 red pepper, cut into 1-inch chunks

1 zucchini, sliced into ¾-inch thick pieces

1 red onion, diced into ¾-inch pieces

Salt and pepper, to taste

Skewers (if using wood, soaked in cold water for 30 minutes before using)

Preparation

Preparation at home

1. Add oyster sauce, soy sauce, 1 tablespoon olive oil, garlic, and sesame oil to a bowl. Mix until well combined. Toss in steak until completely coated on all sides. Cover and store in the refrigerator until you are ready to leave for the trip. Transfer to a sealable container and keep inside a cooler once travelling.

At the campsite

2. Light charcoal briquettes in a chimney starter for about 10 minutes or until gray and ashy. Add charcoal in barbecue pit and place grill to the medium position.

3. In a bowl, add red peppers, zucchini, and red onion. Then, pour in remaining olive oil, salt, and pepper. Toss everything together until mixed and well coated.

4. Take skewers and add strip loin and vegetables in an alternating pattern.

5. Place skewers on grill and cook for about 8 to 10 minutes, rotating a few times to cook evenly.

6. Remove from heat and serve.

Black Rice, Ricotta, and Radishes Salad

This vegetarian dish combines fluffy black rice, tasty dried ricotta, and a mixture of chopped radishes, topped with a delicious vinaigrette, fresh herbs, and almonds.

Serves: 4 – Preparation Time: 5 minutes – Cooking Time: 1 hour

Nutritional facts per serving: calories 400, total fat 23 g, saturated fat 5 g, carbs 44 g, sugar 2 g, fibers 5 g, protein 9 g, sodium 280 mg

Ingredients

¼ cup olive oil

2 tablespoons red wine vinegar

Salt and pepper, to taste

1 cup black rice

1¾ cups water

2 cups mixed radishes, sliced and quartered

2 ounces salted dry ricotta, finely sliced

¼ cup almonds, unsalted and roasted, diced

¼ cup fresh dill, diced

2 tablespoons fresh chives, diced

Preparation

Preparation at home

1. To prepare the vinaigrette, take a sealable container and add oil and vinegar. Sprinkle salt and pepper to season. Place lid and shake until well combined. You can make this up to 3 days ahead. Store inside refrigerator until you are ready for camping trip, then keep in a cooler once traveling.

At the campsite

2. Add rice and water to pot. Add salt to season. Cook over high heat on your camping stove. Once boiling, lower heat and cover with lid. Let simmer for about 45 to 50 minutes until water is absorbed and rice is soft. Remove from heat and let rest for about 10 minutes. Remove lid to allow the steam to escape and for the rice to cool.

3. Once ready to serve, take a large bowl and add rice, radishes, dressing, salt, and pepper. Toss to mix everything together. Next, add ricotta, almonds, dill, and chives. Toss everything again to combine.

4. Serve.

Grilled Kielbasas, Chicken, and Vegetable Foil Packs

Be summer ready with delicious foil pack dish. Packed with sausages, chicken, and a variety of summer vegetables, this one's sure to have you wanting more.

Serves: 8 – Preparation Time: 25 minutes – Cooking Time: 20 minutes

Nutritional facts per serving: calories 490, total fat 32 g, saturated fat 15 g, carbs 27 g, sugar 4 g, fibers 3 g, protein 24 g, sodium 990 mg

Ingredients

1 pound smoked kielbasas sausages, sliced into 1-inch pieces

4 medium potatoes, peeled and chopped into ½-inch cubes

3 cups green cabbage, shredded

1 large sweet onion, halved and sliced

1 medium green pepper, julienned

1 medium sweet red pepper, julienned

1 small zucchini, sliced

1 small yellow summer squash, sliced

1 pound chicken tenderloins, chopped into 1-inch pieces

2 medium tomatoes, sliced into wedges

½ cup butter, sliced into eight cubes

¼ cup Italian salad dressing

Preparation

1. Preheat grill to medium heat.

2. Lay out 8 12-inch long double-layered sheets of thick aluminum foil onto a flat surface.

3. Mix sausage, potatoes, cabbage, onion, peppers, zucchini, squash, and chicken in a bowl. Once combined, lightly toss in tomatoes.

4. Pour mixture onto the center of each foil sheet. Add a cube of butter on top of each. Roll up the edges of each foil sheet and fold at the center to seal tightly.

5. Arrange foil packs onto grill and place lid. Cook for about 20 to 25 minutes until chicken is cooked through and vegetables turn soft.

6. Remove from heat and open foil packs to let the steam escape.

7. Serve with a drizzle of Italian salad dressing on top.

Grilled Cod, Chorizo, and Potato Foil Packs

Cooked over the camping stove and the grill, these delicious foil packs are drizzled with a delicious DIY sunflower seed and lime butter sauce.

Serves: 4 – Preparation Time: 5 minutes – Cooking Time: 45 minutes

Nutritional facts per serving: calories 570, total fat 34 g, saturated fat 12 g, carbs 28 g, sugar 2 g, fibers 3 g, protein 38 g, sodium 300 mg

Ingredients

Sunflower seed-lime butter

2 tablespoons roasted sunflower seeds
1 tablespoon fresh chives, diced
½ teaspoon lime zest
1 tablespoon fresh lime juice
Salt and pepper, to taste
4 tablespoons unsalted butter, softened

Other ingredients

1½ pounds baby potatoes
2 ounces dried Spanish chorizo, casings removed, diced
2 tablespoons olive oil
2 tablespoons vegetable oil
4 6-ounce skinless cod fillets

Preparation

Preparation at home

1. Prepare the sunflower seed-lime butter by combining seeds, chives, lime zest, lime juice, butter, salt, and pepper in a sealable container and store in the refrigerator until you are ready for the camping trip. You can make this up to 3 days ahead. Keep inside a cooler once travelling.

At the campsite

2. Light charcoal briquettes in a chimney starter for about 10 minutes or until gray and ashy. Add charcoal in barbecue pit and place grill to the medium position.

3. Flatten 4 12-inch long sheets of heavy duty foil onto a surface. Distribute even amounts of potatoes and chorizo among each. Drizzle olive oil on top, then sprinkle with salt and pepper. Roll up edges towards the center and fold at the top to seal tightly.

4. Arrange packs on grill and close lid. Cook for about 25 to 35 minutes until potatoes become soft.

5. Place a large pan over medium-high heat on a camping stove. Add vegetable oil. Once hot, place cod fillets in pan. Sprinkle salt and pepper and cook for about 4 minutes or until bottom side turns a light brown. Flip fillet. Sprinkle other side with salt and pepper. Cook for an additional 2 minutes to cook thoroughly. Remove from heat and spread evenly the prepared sunflower seed-lime butter on top of each fish fillet.

6. Remove packs from grill and unfold foil seals. Place cod over potatoes and pour any remaining butter from the pan.

7. Serve.

Tasty Fried Apple and Caramelized Onion Pork Chops

This interesting combination of apples, onions, and pork chops is a must-try for your next camping trip. Plus, it takes only 15 minutes to make!

Serves: 6 – Preparation Time: 3 minutes – Cooking Time: 12 minutes

Nutritional facts per serving: calories 528, total fat 23 g, saturated fat 8 g, carbs 12 g, sugar 9 g, fibers 2 g, protein 64 g, sodium 178 mg

Ingredients

1 tablespoon olive oil

6 thick-sliced pork chops, bone-in

Salt and pepper, to taste

3 apples, cored and sliced

1 medium sweet onion, sliced

Preparation

1. Heat oil in a pan over medium-high heat. Add pork and cook, turning occasionally, until both sides are nicely brown. Then, reduce heat to medium and season with salt and pepper. Add apples and onion slices.

2. Continue to cook everything until pork is cooked thoroughly.

3. Remove from heat and transfer to a plate.

4. Serve.

Dessert Recipes

Grilled S'mores Cones

Have this unique yet appetizing take on the classic s'mores in as quick as 15 minutes.

Serves: 12 – Preparation Time: 5 minutes – Cooking Time: 10 minutes

Nutritional facts per serving: calories 273, total fat 10 g, saturated fat 5 g, carbs 49 g, sugar 35 g, fibers 0 g, protein 4 g, sodium 66 mg

Ingredients

12 waffle cones

1 bag mini marshmallows

12 ounces chocolate chips

Preparation

1. Distribute even amounts of marshmallows and chocolate chips to each waffle cone. Then, wrap each entirely in aluminum foil. Secure any open edges.

2. Away from direct heat, cook on hot grill for about 7 to 10 minutes until heated through.

3. Unwrap and let cool for a few minutes before serving.

Tasty Coal-baked Monkey Bread

This is a simple dessert that's easy to make and is super delicious. You'll be sure to catch everyone having a bite of this one!

Serves: 6 – Preparation Time: 5 minutes – Cooking Time: 10 minutes

Nutritional facts per serving: calories 452, total fat 17 g, saturated fat 10 g, carbs 74 g, sugar 33 g, fibers 1 g, protein 7 g, sodium 827 mg

Ingredients

1 can refrigerated buttermilk biscuit dough, chopped into quarters

2 tablespoons cinnamon

½ cup white sugar

1 stick butter

½ cup brown sugar

Preparation

1. Completely wrap the inside of your Dutch oven with thick aluminum foil. Then, coat foil with butter to grease.

2. Add cinnamon sugar into a Ziploc bag. Seal tightly and shake to mix thoroughly. Working in batches, drop chopped biscuits into seasoning bag and lightly shake to coat. Transfer coated biscuits into prepared Dutch oven.

3. On your camping stove or campfire, melt butter n a pan. Mix in brown sugar until blended. Remove from heat and add to Dutch oven, pouring mixture over biscuits.

4. Add a sheet of aluminum foil on top of Dutch oven to prevent any ashes from getting to the food. Then, cover with the lid.

5. Bake in hot coals for about 5 to 10 minutes until cooked thoroughly and biscuits are fluffy. Remove from heat.

6. Allow to cool for a few minutes before serving.

Chocolate Chip and Marshmallow Bananas

All you need for this delicious yet simple dessert are bananas, chocolate chips, and mini marshmallows.

Serves: 2 – Preparation Time: 2 minutes – Cooking Time: 5 minutes

Nutritional facts per serving: calories 253, total fat 14 g, saturated fat 5 g, carbs 37 g, sugar 27 g, fibers 3 g, protein 2 g, sodium 8 mg

Ingredients

2 bananas, unpeeled

¼ cup semisweet chocolate chips

¼ cup mini marshmallows

Preparation

1. Make a lengthwise slit through each banana, with the peel, without cutting either end. Gently spread the bananas apart and insert half of the marshmallows and chocolate chips into each of the slits.

2. Cover each banana entirely in aluminum foil, securing any open edges. Cook over the campfire for about 5 minutes until marshmallows are gooey and chocolate chips are melted.

3. Serve.

Toasted Fruit-filled Pie Sandwiches

Make your very own delicious pies in the woods with this simple yet versatile dish. Fill them with whatever fruit you want—cherries, blueberries, peaches… you name it!

Serves: 4 – Preparation Time: 5 minutes – Cooking Time: 5 minutes

Nutritional facts per serving: calories 129, total fat 1 g, saturated fat 0 g, carbs 29 g, sugar 17 g, fibers 2 g, protein 3 g, sodium 123 mg

Ingredients

Non-stick cooking spray

8 bread slices

4 teaspoons cinnamon-sugar mixture

16 to 24 tablespoons preferred fruit

Preparation

1. Heat coals in your campfire or a chimney starter until coals are very hot and glowing.

2. Coat inner sides of camp cooker with non-stick cooking spray, then place a bread slice onto each side. Apply pressure to the center of both slices to create a depression in the bread. Fill the depression with about 2 to 3 tablespoons fruit with 1 teaspoon cinnamon-sugar mixture. Close the camp cooker and cut off any excess bread that is outside of the vessel. Repeat for remaining pies.

3. Cook directly in campfire at the hottest part for about 2 to 3 minutes until both sides of the bread slices are toasted and lightly brown.

4. Remove from heat and transfer pies to a serving platter. Let cool for a minute or two before serving.

Coconut Golden Oreo S'mores

This adorable dessert takes less than 5 minutes to make and requires only 2 simple ingredients: Golden Oreos and coconut marshmallows.

Serves: 3 – Preparation Time: 1 minute – Cooking Time: 1 minute

Nutritional facts per serving: calories 88, total fat 3 g, saturated fat 1 g, carbs 15 g, sugar 9 g, fibers 0 g, protein 1 g, sodium 46 mg

Ingredients

3 coconut marshmallows

3 Golden Oreos

Preparation

1. Toast marshmallows over campfire until toasted and gooey.

2. Twist open each Golden Oreo and sandwich marshmallows in between the two cookies. Repeat with each cookie.

3. Serve.

6-minute Camping Éclairs

You won't believe how simple this version of the classic French dessert is to make. And it only takes all of 6 minutes, too!

Serves: 6 – Preparation Time: 1 minute – Cooking Time: 5 minutes

Nutritional facts per serving: calories 111, total fat 6 g, saturated fat 2 g, carbs 12 g, sugar 4 g, fibers 0 g, protein 1 g, sodium 128 mg

Ingredients

Canola oil

1 tube refrigerated crescent rolls, cut into 6 squares

6 snack pack-sized vanilla pudding

6 tablespoons chocolate frosting

Whipped cream spray

Preparation

1. Brush end of wooden sticks or dowels with oil, then attach each crescent roll square onto each wooden stick by coiling it around the end. Lightly press end of dough onto overlapping dough to secure in place

2. Toast dough over hot coals, rotating to make sure they cook evenly, until lightly brown and a bit crisp.

3. Remove from heat and gently pull the cooked dough from the sticks. When cooled cut in half but not the whole way through. fill insides with vanilla pudding. Spread chocolate frosting on top and add a dollup of whipped cream.

4. Serve.

Camping Cinnamon Roll Skewers

Enjoy this campfire-cooked cinnamon-flavored pastry dessert in just 10 quick minutes.

Serves: 6 – Preparation Time: 5 minutes – Cooking Time: 5 minutes

Nutritional facts per serving: calories 99, total fat 3 g, saturated fat 1 g, carbs 19 g, sugar 14 g, fibers 1 g, protein 1 g, sodium 85 mg

Ingredients

1 tablespoon cinnamon

¼ cup sugar

1 package crescent rolls, separated into 6 pieces

¼ cup powdered sugar

2 to 3 tablespoons water

Preparation

1. In a bowl or Ziploc bag, add cinnamon and sugar. Mix well until incorporated.

2. Next, wrap each crescent roll piece onto a skewer, then evenly coat them in the prepared cinnamon-sugar mixture.

3. Toast over campfire, while rotating to cook evenly, for about 5 minutes. Remove from heat.

4. While rolls are cooling, make the glaze by combining powdered sugar and water in a bowl.

5. Add a drizzle of prepared glaze on top of rolls.

6. Serve.

Blueberry Muffins in Orange Peel Cups

These tasty campfire-cooked blueberry muffins use orange skins instead of muffin trays. They add a great citrusy flavor and look super cute, too!

Serves: 4 – Preparation Time: 5 minutes – Cooking Time: 10 minutes

Nutritional facts per serving: calories 385, total fat 5 g, saturated fat 1 g, carbs 78 g, sugar 38 g, fibers 0 g, protein 6 g, sodium 557 mg

Ingredients

1 box blueberry muffin mix

4 oranges, cut in half and flesh scooped out

Preparation

1. Prepare blueberry muffin mix based on package instructions.
2. Place a few tablespoons muffin mix into each of the orange halves, then put two halves together to make a ball. Completely cover all oranges in a triple layer of aluminum foil.
3. Cook foil wraps directly in campfire for about 10-12 minutes, rotating often to cook evenly. They are ready once muffins are cooked and set all the way through. Open one packet to check for doneness. A fork inserted in the muffin should come out clean. If not continue cooking for 1-3 minutes more.
4. Remove aluminum foil wraps from oranges and serve.

Dutch Oven Fruit Cobbler

You can choose whatever type of fruit you have with you (or can find) while camping for this amazing and effortless fruit cobbler.

Serves: 4 – Preparation Time: 1 minute – Cooking Time: 30 minutes

Nutritional facts per serving: calories 793, total fat 7 g, saturated fat 2 g, carbs 182 g, sugar 66 g, fibers 7 g, protein 8 g, sodium 829 mg

Ingredients

1 box yellow cake mix

2 30-ounce canned fruit of choice

1 can Sprite

Preparation

1. Add yellow cake mix, fruit, and sprite to a bowl and mix until smooth. Add batter to a Dutch oven lined with aluminum foil.
2. Make a ring of hot coals that's just about the same circumference as your Dutch oven, then place it on top. Cover with lid, then top with a few more hot coals. Bake for about 30 minutes. Check for doneness by inserting a fork. It should come out clean without trace of wet batter.
3. Remove from heat and serve.

Dark Chocolate S'mores with Hazelnut and Blackberries

This is a delicious take on the classic S'mores using dark chocolate with hazelnuts, plus a few blackberries.

Serves: 4 – Preparation Time: 5 minutes – Cooking Time: 5 minutes

Nutritional facts per serving: calories 99, total fat 3 g, saturated fat 1 g, carbs 17 g, sugar 8 g, fibers 2 g, protein 1 g, sodium 37 mg

Ingredients

4 marshmallow

4 graham cracker, halved

4 square dark chocolate with hazelnut

12 blackberries

Preparation

1. Pierce marshmallows through skewers and toast over the campfire until nicely charred.

2. To assemble each S'more, take 1graham cracker half and layer chocolate, toasted marshmallow, blackberries, and top with remaining graham cracker half.

3. Serve.

Coal-baked Cinnamon Roll Apple Pie

This camping-friendly apple pie is made with chopped up cinnamon rolls, baked in between hot coals, and drizzled with a cream cheese and caramel icing.

Serves: 12 – Preparation Time: 20 minutes – Cooking Time: 30 minutes

Nutritional facts per serving: calories 432, total fat 17 g, saturated fat 3 g, carbs 68 g, sugar 43 g, fibers 4 g, protein 6 g, sodium 412 mg

Ingredients

Non-stick cooking spray

12 refrigerated cinnamon rolls, cut into 4 pieces

2 Granny Smith apples, peeled and cubed

½ cup brown sugar

1 teaspoon cinnamon

½ cup graham cracker crumbs

¼ cup pecans, diced

2 packets cream cheese frosting

⅓ cup caramel ice cream topping

Preparation

1. Coat a 12-inch Dutch oven with non-stick cooking spray. Line cinnamon roll pieces on the bottom of the Dutch oven. Let rest, with cover, for about 1 to 2 hours to rise.

2. Meanwhile, add apples, brown sugar, cinnamon, graham, and pecans to a bowl. Mix well until combined. Once rolls are ready, take off cover and top with prepared mixture.

3. Return lid and put Dutch oven over hot coals. Arrange additionalhot coals evenly on the cover. Bake for about 45 minutes.

4. As pie cooks, mix cream cheese and caramel topping in a bowl.

5. Once cooked, top pie with a drizzle of cream cheese-caramel mixture. Serve warm.

Grilled Sweet Potatoes with Marshmallow and Pecans

Grilled on a cast iron pan, this tasty sweet potato dessert becomes even tastier and sweeter with marshmallow fluff, brown sugar, cinnamon, pecans, and lots of butter.

Serves: 8-12 – Preparation Time: 15 minutes – Cooking Time: 2 hours

Nutritional facts per serving: calories 224, total fat 15 g, saturated fat 8 g, carbs 23 g, sugar 13 g, fibers 3 g, protein 2 g, sodium 107 mg

Ingredients

4 large sweet potatoes, cut into ⅛-inch slices but not all the way through

½ cup butter (1stick)

1 teaspoon cinnamon, ground

⅛ teaspoon ground clove

¼ teaspoon ground allspice

Salt, to taste

⅓ cup marshmallow fluff

¼ cup brown sugar

⅓ cup chopped pecans

Preparation

1. Preheat grill to 400 °F.

2. In a cast iron Dutch oven, let butter melt. Stir-in cinnamon, cloves, and allspice. Remove from heat.

3. Pace the Sweet potatoes in the Dutch oven. Season with salt and pepper. Drizzle 2 tablespoons of the melted and seasoned butter on top of each.

4. Transfer Dutch oven onto grill and close lid. Cook for about 30 minutes over indirect heat.

5. Remove lid. Hold pan and tilt to let the butter slide to one side. Baste potatoes with butter. Close lid again and continue cooking for about 1 hour and 15 minutes more or until potatoes are tender. Keep basting potatoes every 20 to 30 minutes.

6. Remove lid and spread marshmallow fluff on top of each potato, followed by brown sugar and pecans. Let cook for an additional 5 minutes. Spoon butter on top one last time before removing from grill.

7. Serve.

Orange Caramel Brownie Muffins

Cooked directly in your campfire, these delicious muffins combine the wonderful taste of brownies and the citrusy taste of oranges.

Serves: 8 – Preparation Time: 10 minutes – Cooking Time: 40 minutes

Nutritional facts per serving: calories 206, total fat 3 g, saturated fat 1 g, carbs 36 g, sugar 20 g, fibers 1 g, protein 1 g, sodium 149 mg

Ingredients

1 box brownie mix

8 whole oranges, sliced horizontally 1½ inches off the top and hollowed out

Corn flakes cereal, crushed

Caramel sauce

Preparation

1. Prepare the brownie batter according to the instructions on the package.

2. Pour prepared batter into each of the hollowed out oranges. Leave about 1 inch from the top unfilled. Cover each with sliced off orange peel as a lid.

3. Wrap each in 2 layers of thick aluminum foil

4. Arrange foil packs in your campfire. Let cook for about 30 to 50 minutes, depending on the intensity of your campfire. Make sure to rotate the foil packs often so they cook evenly.

5. Carefully open up foil packs. Remove orange peel lid and sprinkle crushed cereal on top. Finish with a drizzle of caramel sauce.

6. Serve.

Grilled One Pan Chocolate and Berry Pound Cake

This is a refreshing and simple dessert that consist of a mixture of chocolate, pound cake, and mixed berries. Everyone's going to want seconds.

Serves: 6 – Preparation Time: 10 minutes – Cooking Time: 10 minutes

Nutritional facts per serving: calories 353, total fat 17 g, saturated fat 8 g, carbs 45 g, sugar 4 g, fibers 6 g, protein 4 g, sodium 281 mg

Ingredients

12 ounces fresh berries

2 tablespoons sugar

¼ cup butter

¾ pounds pound cake, cut into 1-inch cubes

2 packs chocolate bars, cut into small squares

Preparation

1. In a bowl, add berries and sugar. Mix and set aside for about 10 to 15 minutes until juices begin to release.

2. Heat butter in a cast iron pan over camping grill. Once melted, add pound cake pieces. Stir to make sure to evenly toasted on all sides. Remove from heat.

3. Add berries and chocolate evenly over the cake pieces. Cover with lid or aluminum foil and set aside for about 5 to 10 minutes to allow berries to become warm and for chocolate to melt.

4. Remove cover and serve.

One Pan Chocolate Chip Cookie

Who says you can't make homemade cookies at camp? Whip up this delicious all-time favorite dessert with a grill, cast iron pan, and a few ingredients.

Serves: 8 – Preparation Time: 10 minutes – Cooking Time: 20 minutes

Nutritional facts per serving: calories 617, total fat 38 g, saturated fat 22 g, carbs 80 g, sugar 74 g, fibers 1 g, protein 5 g, sodium 625 mg

Ingredients

1 cup softened butter or margarine

1 cup brown sugar, packed

1 cup sugar

2 eggs

1 teaspoon vanilla

3 cups flour

½ cup oats, quick cooking

1 teaspoon sea salt

¾ teaspoon baking soda

1½ cups chocolate chips

Preparation

1. Set camping grill to 350 °F.

2. In a large bowl, add butter and whisk until smooth. Then, add sugars and mix until fluffy. Mix in eggs and vanilla until well combined.

3. Add flour, oats, salt, and baking soda. Mix well until combined. Add chocolate chips and stir until incorporated.

4. Pour mixture into a large cast iron pan and place onto grill.

5. Cover and cook for about 20 minutes until cooked through and golden brown.

6. Remove from heat and serve.

Fried Apple Pie Bread Rolls

Who needs an oven when you can make delicious fun-size apple pies with your camping stove? Have this delicious dessert ready in less than 20 minutes.

Serves: 4 – Preparation Time: 15 minutes – Cooking Time: 4 minutes

Nutritional facts per serving: calories 389, total fat 5 g, saturated fat 2 g, carbs 8 g, sugar 57 g, fibers 3 g, protein 7 g, sodium 286 mg

Ingredients

12 slices white bread, flattened and crust removed

1 can apple pie filling

2 eggs

3 tablespoons milk

1 dash vanilla

½ cup granulated sugar

2 teaspoons cinnamon, ground

2 tablespoons butter

Preparation

1. Coat one side of each flattened bread slice with about 2 tablespoons apple pie filling. Then, from edge to edge, roll up each bread slice. Secure with toothpick.

2. In a bowl, combine eggs, milk, and vanilla. Then, in a separate bowl, mix together sugar and cinnamon.

3. Heat butter in a pan over medium heat.

4. Lightly soak each roll into prepared egg mixture to coat entirely, then arrange into pan and remove toothpicks.

5. Cook, turning often to cook evenly on all sides, until lightly browned.

6. Quickly transfer rolls into the sugar and cinnamon mixture. Toss to coat evenly all over.

7. Serve.

Grilled Peach and Pecans with a Caramel Sauce

With sliced peaches and pecans, caramel sauce, and some brown sugar, this is a light and delicious dessert you can have in just 30 minutes.

Serves: 2 – Preparation Time: 5 minutes – Cooking Time: 25 minutes

Nutritional facts per serving: calories 204, total fat 13 g, saturated fat 2 g, carbs 24 g, sugar 10 g, fibers 3 g, protein 2 g, sodium 46 mg

Ingredients

1 teaspoon butter

1 tablespoon brown sugar

1 tablespoon caramel sauce

¼ cup pecans, halved

2 ripe peaches, pits removed and sliced in half

Preparation

1. Preheat grill to low heat.

2. Lay out a 6-inch square piece of aluminum foil onto a flat surface. Coat with butter and sprinkle 1 tablespoon brown sugar evenly on top. Then, distribute pecans all over the sheet on top of the sugar.

3. Arrange peach halves over the pecans. Make sure you place them sliced side down. Evenly pour caramel sauce over top.

4. Fold foil sheets to wrap peaches and secure edges together to seal.

5. Place onto grill and cook for about 20 to 25 minutes.

6. Remove from grill and open up foil pack to cool.

7. Transfer to a plate and serve once slightly cooled but still warm.

Stuffed Coal-Roasted Apples

This is a quick and easy dessert that is made up of softened, coal-cooked apples stuffed with a mixture of nuts, berries, and a few other delicious ingredients.

Serves: 4 – Preparation Time: 15 minutes – Cooking Time: 20 minutes

Nutritional facts per serving: calories 217, total fat 15 g, saturated fat 7 g, carbs 24 g, sugar 17 g, fibers 4 g, protein 1 g, sodium 42 mg

Ingredients

4 small apples, cored and halved

2 tablespoons butter, softened

1 tablespoon coconut oil

1 tablespoon brown sugar

¼ teaspoon cinnamon

2 tablespoons dried cranberries

3 tablespoons oats

Small handful pecans, halved

Preparation

1. Add butter, coconut oil, brown sugar, and cinnamon in a bowl. Mix well until combined. Then, fold in cranberries, oats, and pecans.

2. Lay out 4 sheets of aluminum foil onto a flat surface. Coat each side of apple halves with prepared mixture. Combine each apple half with their respective apple half, like a sandwich. Place each onto the center of 1 foil sheet and wrap completely.

3. Arrange foil wraps in hot coals and cook for about 15 to 20 minutes until soft.

4. Remove from heat and let cool without removing foil for 5minutes before serving.

Mini Campfire Dessert Pizzas

This is a super tasty and sweet pizza that you can make on the grill in less than 15 minutes.

Serves: 8 – Preparation Time: 3 minutes – Cooking Time: 10 minutes

Nutritional facts per serving: calories 270, total fat 15 g, saturated fat 6 g, carbs 28 g, sugar 5 g, fibers 3 g, protein 9 g, sodium 302 mg

Ingredients

Vegetable oil, for brushing

10 ounces ricotta cheese

Any liquid sweetener, a few drops to taste

1 dash pure vanilla extract

1 pound pizza dough, divided into 8 pieces

1 cup fresh cherries, pitted

2 ounces dark chocolate, chopped

3 ounces pecans, chopped

Preparation

1. Coat camping grill grates with oil, then set to medium-high heat.

2. In a bowl, add ricotta cheese, liquid sweetener, and vanilla extract. Mix well until combined.

3. Take each pizza dough portion and roll them out until each is a ¼-inch thick disk. Brush each side with oil.

4. Arrange disks onto grill and cook for about 2 minutes per side until disks puff up. Lower heat to medium. Turn disks over and continue cooking for about 1 minute. Remove from heat.

5. Layer each pizza with ricotta, cherries, chocolate, and nuts. Then, return pizzas to grill. Cook, with lid closed, for 2 to 3 minutes or until chocolate melts.

6. Serve.

One-Pan Three-Berry Cobbler

This is an amazing dessert to prepare if you have the chance to go berry picking near your campsite. Cooked over the campfire, this mixed berry cobbler is great for sharing.

Serves: 8 – Preparation Time: 10 minutes – Cooking Time: 35 minutes

Nutritional facts per serving: calories 181, total fat 3 g, saturated fat 2 g, carbs 37 g, sugar 17 g, fibers 6 g, protein 3 g, sodium 182 mg

Ingredients

2 pounds fresh mixed berries (blueberries, raspberries and blackberries)

¼ cup plus 2 tablespoons and 1 teaspoon sugar, divided

2 tablespoons water

1 tablespoon fresh lemon juice

1 cup all-purpose flour

1 teaspoon baking powder

½ teaspoon baking soda

¼ teaspoon coarse salt

½ cup plus 2 tablespoons buttermilk

2 tablespoons unsalted butter, melted

⅛ teaspoon cinnamon, ground

Preparation

1. In a cast iron skillet, add berries, ¼ cup sugar, water, and lemon juice. Stir and cook over the campfire for about 10 to 15 minutes until mixture thickens.

2. Mix flour, baking powder, baking soda, salt, and 2 tablespoons sugar in a bowl. Pour in buttermilk and butter. Mix until combined and the mixture turns into a tacky dough.

3. In a separate bowl, combine cinnamon and 1 teaspoon sugar to make the cinnamon-sugar spice.

4. Add 6 heaping spoonfuls of dough onto the berries, then distribute cinnamon-sugar spice evenly on top.

5. Cover with lid or loosely with foil. Continue cooking for about 20 minutes until cooked through. Insert a toothpick in the cobbler cake, when cooked it should come out clean, if not continue cooking for another 2-3 minutes

6. Serve.

Snacks/Sides Recipes

Campfire-toasted Breadsticks on Sticks

This flavorful breadstick may not exactly be shaped like a stick, but it was cooked wrapped around one. That counts, right?

Serves: 6 – Preparation Time: 2 minutes – Cooking Time: 5 minutes

Nutritional facts per serving: calories 80, total fat 2 g, saturated fat 1 g, carbs 14 g, sugar 2 g, fibers 1 g, protein 2 g, sodium 258 mg

Ingredients

1 tube breadstick dough

Butter

1 pinch garlic powder

1 pinch salt

1 pinch oregano

1 pinch rosemary

1 pinch thyme

1 pinch Cajun seasoning

Preparation

1. Flatten dough onto a smooth, clean surface. Divide into 6 pieces, then wrap each onto a wooden dowel or stick. Lightly press the end of each dough onto the overlapping dough to secure in place.

2. Prepare seasoning by combining garlic powder, salt, oregano, rosemary, thyme, and Cajun seasoning in a bowl or Ziploc bag. Set aside.

3. Cook dough over campfire, rotating every now and then to cook evenly, until toasted to your liking.

4. Remove from heat and brush with butter. Dredge in prepared seasoning mix. Serve warm.

Chili Cheese Fries Camping Snack

Cook these delicious chili cheese fries, wrapped with aluminum foil, over the campfire.

Serves: 4 – Preparation Time: 1 minute – Cooking Time: 25 minutes

Nutritional facts per serving: calories 347, total fat 21 g, saturated fat 10 g, carbs 24 g, sugar 0 g, fibers 2 g, protein 17 g, sodium 611 mg

Ingredients

Non-stick cooking spray

1 small package frozen French fries

1 can chili

1 cup cheddar cheese, grated

Preparation

1. Layer 2 sheets of aluminum foil one on top of the other. Then, coat top layer with non-stick cooking spray.

2. Add fries onto the center of the foil. Fold up sides towards the center and roll together to securely close foil pack.

3. Place foil pack on a grill grate over your campfire and cook for about 15 to 20 minutes. Unroll top of foil packet and add chili and cheese on top of the fries. Reroll to close and cook until cheese is gooey and melted.

4. Remove from heat. Open up foil packs and let cool for a few minutes before serving.

Sautéed Gourmet Mushrooms

Cooked over the campfire, this side dish uses a combination of delicious ingredients to make it more than just your average mushroom side.

Serves: 4 – Preparation Time: 5 minutes – Cooking Time: 20 minutes

Nutritional facts per serving: calories 200, total fat 16 g, saturated fat 7 g, carbs 9 g, sugar 0 g, fibers 2 g, protein 5 g, sodium 20 mg

Ingredients

2 tablespoons olive oil

3 tablespoons butter

2 small shallots, finely sliced

2 garlic cloves, finely sliced

1 sprig fresh rosemary

1 pound cremini mushrooms, cleaned and cut into thirds

¼ pound Portobello mushroom, cleaned and cut into thick slices

½ lemon, juice only

¼ cup red wine

¼ pound morels, end trimmed

Preparation

1. Make your campfire using coals and add a grill grate on top. Add a cast iron skillet over grill grate and heat olive oil and butter in pan until melted.

2. Sauté shallots in skillet for about 1 minute, then mix in garlic, rosemary, and cremini mushrooms. Sauté for about 3 minutes or until tender. Next, add portabella mushrooms and sauté for another 3 to 5 minutes. Pour in lemon juice and cook, stirring, for about 1 minute. Drizzle wine and cook for 5 minutes more. Lastly, mix in morels and move pan to a less hot part of fire. Heat for about 3 minutes.

3. Serve as a side dish.

Toasted Mustard-coated Brussels Sprouts

If you want to try a healthier snack for your next camping trip, this Brussels sprouts dish is a must-try.

Serves: 4 – Preparation Time: 5 minutes – Cooking Time: 10 minutes

Nutritional facts per serving: calories 110, total fat 8 g, saturated fat 1 g, carbs 9 g, sugar 2 g, fibers 3 g, protein 3 g, sodium 99 mg

Ingredients

1 pound Brussels sprouts

Water for boiling

Ice and water for cooling bath

2 tablespoons whole grain mustard

2 tablespoons olive oil

Salt and pepper, to taste

Preparation

1. Boil Brussels sprouts in a large pot for about 3 to 4 minutes. Drain well, then transfer to a bowl filled with ice and water. Afterwards, remove from water and dry using a clean cloth or paper towel. Cut off bottom stems and outer leaves. Set aside.

2. Next, combine mustard, olive oil, salt, and pepper in a bowl. Add prepared sprouts to bowl and toss to coat in mustard mixture. Set aside to marinate for about 30 minutes.

3. Once ready to cook, preheat grill. Place marinated sprouts through skewers with about 3 to 4 sprouts per skewer.

4. Cook on hot grill for about 3 to 5 minutes until toasted well. Rotate skewers halfway through. Remove from grill and coat with another layer of prepared mustard mixture.

5. Serve.

Cheese and Spinach Dip Foil Packet

You can count on this deliciously cheesy spinach dip to make your snack even tastier.

Serves: 6 – Preparation Time: 5 minutes – Cooking Time: 25 minutes

Nutritional facts per serving: calories 194, total fat 17 g, saturated fat 10 g, carbs 4 g, sugar 1 g, fibers 1 g, protein 8 g, sodium 311 mg

Ingredients

1 cup sour cream

1 package cream cheese, softened

¾ cup Parmesan cheese, grated

¾ cup frozen spinach, drained and chopped

Preparation

1. Prepare dip ahead of time. Combine sour cream, cream cheese, Parmesan cheese, and spinach in a container with a secure lid. Keep refrigerated for at least 4 to 6 hours before using.

2. Once at campsite and ready to serve dip, place 2 sheets of aluminum foil one on top of the other to create a double-layered sheet. Next, scoop prepared mixture onto the middle of the sheet. Fold edges towards the center and roll together to close securely, forming a tight ball.

3. Place foil packet near hot coals, but away from direct fire, for about 20 to 25 minutes until heated through.

4. Unroll seal and serve as a dip.

Coconut and Curry Noodle Soup

Warm yourself up during those unexpectedly rainy camping days with this soothing and super easy coconut- and curry-flavored noodle soup.

Serves: 1 – Preparation Time: 5 minutes – Cooking Time: 2 minutes

Nutritional facts per serving: calories 482, total fat 26 g, saturated fat 20 g, carbs 53 g, sugar 6 g, fibers 3 g, protein 7 g, sodium 3385 mg

Ingredients

½ packet coconut cream powder

1 to 2 cubes vegetable bouillon

1 teaspoon curry powder

1 pinch cayenne pepper

2 cups water

1 handful rice noodles

1 handful dehydrated vegetables of choice

Preparation

1. Mix together coconut cream powder, bouillon, curry powder, and cayenne in a bowl or Ziploc bag. Set aside.

2. Next, bring water to a boil in a pot. Add noodles and dehydrated vegetables to boiling water and cook until noodles and vegetables are soft and cooked through.

3. Pour in prepared mixture and stir until dissolved.

4. Serve.

Corn Chip Nacho Bags

This corn chip dish makes a simple and easy-to-eat snack you can enjoy while walking in the outdoors.

Serves: 5 – Preparation Time: 10 minutes – Cooking Time: 30 minutes

Nutritional facts per serving: calories 541, total fat 36 g, saturated fat 11 g, carbs 33 g, sugar 3 g, fibers 5 g, protein 21 g, sodium 974 mg

Ingredients

1 pound ground beef

1 packet chili seasoning mix

¼ teaspoon pepper

1 10-ounce can tomatoes and green chilies, chopped

1 15-ounce can pinto beans in tomato sauce

5 1-ounce bags corn chips

Cheddar cheese, grated

Sour cream

Scallions, chopped

Preparation

1. Cook beef in a pan over medium heat for 6 to 8 minutes until brown, breaking apart meat as you cook. Remove any excess liquid. Then, add chili seasoning mix, pepper, tomatoes, and beans. Mix well and bring to a boil. Lower heat or move off direct heat once boiling and let simmer for about 20 to 25 minutes. Stir from time to time as mixture cooks.

2. When ready to serve, open corn chip bags and spoon as much beef mixture, cheddar cheese, sour cream, and scallions as you would prefer into the bags.

3. Serve.

Mexican-style Grilled Corn

This toasted corn on the cob makes for a great cheese-coated snack with just the perfect amount of spiciness.

Serves: 6 – Preparation Time: 10 minutes – Cooking Time: 20 minutes

Nutritional facts per serving: calories 243, total fat 16 g, saturated fat 5 g, carbs 18 g, sugar 3 g, fibers 2 g, protein 10 g, sodium 485 mg

Ingredients

6 ears corn, with husks

Water for soaking

⅓ cup mayonnaise

2 tablespoons sour cream

½ teaspoon ground poblano chili pepper, plus more for serving

2 teaspoons fresh lime juice

1 pinch salt

1 cup Parmesan cheese

Lime wedges

Preparation

1. Loosen husks from corn, but do not take completely off. Place corn in cold water for about 20 minutes to soak.

2. Meanwhile, preheat camp grill to medium-hot which is about 350 °F.

3. Once corn is done soaking, pull back husks and take out strands of silk attached to kernels. Return husks to cover corn. Then, loosely tie a cooking twine around the corn.

4. Arrange corn on grill, then cover. Grill for about 20 minutes, flipping corn in 5-minute intervals to cook each evenly.

Remove corn from heat once kernels become soft. Make sure not to overcook as this will result in mushy kernels.

5. While corn is cooking combine mayonnaise, sour cream, poblano chili pepper, lime juice, and salt to make the spread. Mix well.

6. Sprinkle Parmesan onto a plate.

7. Once corn is cooked, remove husks and coat prepared spread onto corn using a brush. Then, coat corn with Parmesan cheese by rolling each cob onto the plate.

8. Serve with a drizzle of lime wedges on top followed by a sprinkle of more poblano chili pepper.

All-Dressed Cheese Nachos Skillet

Can't decide if you want nachos or pizza for snacks? With this pizza nachos snack, you and your friends can have both at the same time. Yum!

Serves: 6 – Preparation Time: 5 minutes – Cooking Time: 15 minutes

Nutritional facts per serving: calories 482, total fat 36 g, saturated fat 16 g, carbs 28 g, sugar 1 g, fibers 3 g, protein 14 g, sodium 868 mg

Ingredients

1½ tablespoons unsalted butter

½ tablespoons olive oil

3 cloves garlic, finely chopped

½ cup heavy cream

¼ cup milk

Salt and pepper, to taste

Red pepper flakes, to taste

¼ cup Parmesan cheese

1 bag tortilla chips

¼ cup onion, chopped

½ cup pepperoni, quartered

½ cup black olives, sliced

½ bell pepper, chopped

2 scallions, sliced

1 cup jack cheese, grated

Preparation

1. First, prepare the garlic cream sauce by adding butter and olive oil to a saucepan. Heat until butter is melted, then toss in garlic. Cook for about 1 to 2 minutes, then stir in cream and milk. While stirring, bring to a boil. Mix in salt, pepper, red pepper flakes, and cheese until mixture thickens. Remove from heat.

2. For the nachos, put tortilla chips into a pan and lightly pour ½ cups prepared garlic cream sauce evenly on top. Next, layer onions, pepperoni, olives, bell pepper, and jack cheese on top.

3. Transfer pan over campfire grate and place lid. Heat for about 5 to 8 minutes until cheese begins to bubble and vegetables are heated through.

4. Serve.

Coal-baked Campfire Potatoes

This is an easy side dish to prepare for lunch or dinner. Cook this while you're preparing the main meal and you'll have a complete meal in no time.

Serves: 8 – Preparation Time: 5 minutes – Cooking Time: 45 minutes

Nutritional facts per serving: calories 163, total fat 3 g, saturated fat 1 g, carbs 32 g, sugar 2 g, fibers 3 g, protein 4 g, sodium 42 mg

Ingredients

4 large Russet potatoes

Oil

Salt and pepper, to taste

Preparation

1. Thoroughly scrub each potato to make remove any dirt. Pat dry with a paper towel, then apply a bit of oil onto each.

2. Take 4 double-layered sheets of aluminum foil and wrap each potato individually. Twist the ends of the foil sheets to seal and to make handles to hold the packs with later.

3. Remove a few hot coals from your campfire and put them to one side. Place foil-wrapped potatoes into hot coals, making sure that coals are around potatoes and not just under them. Leave to bake for about 45 minutes until potatoes are tender. Turn potatoes every 20 minutes to cook each side evenly. Remove from heat.

4. Remove foil carefully since these would be very hot. Halve potatoes lengthwise, then season with salt and pepper.

5. Serve.

Campfire-popped Cheese Popcorn Foil Pack

This is a quick and easy snack to munch on while having those late night conversations around the campfire.

Serves: 2 – Preparation Time: 5 minutes – Cooking Time: 10 minutes

Nutritional facts per serving: calories 71, total fat 7 g, saturated fat 1 g, carbs 1 g, sugar 0 g, fibers 0 g, protein 1 g, sodium 101 mg

Ingredients

¼ cup popcorn kernels, uncooked

1 tablespoon canola oil

½ tablespoon Parmesan cheese

Salt, to taste

Preparation

1. Lay out 1 18-inch long sheet of aluminum foil and place popcorn kernels in the center. Lightly pour oil all over top. Then, fold edges of the sheet towards the center and seal at the top. Make sure you leave extra room inside the foil pack for when the kernels pop.

2. Using long tongs, cook kernel packet over your campfire for about 3 to 5 minutes until they begin to pop. Lightly shake over fire for about 2 to 3 minutes until the popping stops.

3. Remove from heat and unseal foil pack. Season with salt and sprinkle Parmesan on top. Toss together to coat thoroughly.

4. Serve.

Grilled Bacon-wrapped Onion Rings with a Spicy Lime Dipping Sauce

This is a delicious snack to prepare during an afternoon rest after a full morning of outdoor activities.

Serves: 3-4 – Preparation Time: 15 minutes – Cooking Time: 1 hour 30 minutes

Nutritional facts per serving: calories 261, total fat 14 g, saturated fat 4 g, carbs 20 g, sugar 13 g, fibers 3 g, protein 14 g, sodium 807 mg

Ingredients

½ pound bacon strips

2 large sweet onions, cut into ½-inch thick rings and separate

Black pepper

¼ cup hot sauce

Dipping sauce

½ cup mayonnaise

1 tablespoon hot sauce, more if you like it spicier

1 teaspoon lime juice

Preparation

1. Preheat camping grill to 350 °F.

2. Coat onion rings with hot sauce, then coil each ring with bacon. Pierce a toothpick through each to keep bacon in place while cooking. Next, season onions with black pepper.

3. Arrange onion rings onto grill for indirect heat. Close lid, and cook for about 1 hour and 30 minutes, turning over every 20-30 minutes.

4. Prepare dipping sauce by mixing mayonnaise, 1 tablespoon hot sauce, and lime juice in a bowl.

5. Remove rings from heat and serve with prepared dipping sauce on the side.

Grilled Lemon Zucchini Strips

Cooked over the grill, you won't be able to get enough of this delicious well-seasoned zucchini snack topped with lemon zest and a bit of salt.

Serves: 8 – Preparation Time: 30 minutes – Cooking Time: 20 minutes

Nutritional facts per serving: calories 90, total fat 7 g, saturated fat 1 g, carbs 8 g, sugar 3 g, fibers 3 g, protein 1 g, sodium 587 mg

Ingredients

6 medium zucchinis, ends trimmed, quartered lengthwise

¼ cup olive oil

1 tablespoon plus 1 teaspoon kosher salt, plus more if needed

1 teaspoon ground black pepper

3 lemons, zest grated

Preparation

1. In a large Ziploc bag, add zucchini, olive oil, 1 teaspoon salt, pepper, 1 tablespoon lemon zest, and juice of 2 lemons. Seal tightly. Then, using your hands, massage ingredients together until zucchini is well coated. Put to the side for about 20 minutes to marinate.

2. Preheat grill to medium-low heat. Once ready, arrange zucchini onto grill and cook for about 20 minutes, turning over to cook each side evenly, until tender. Remove from heat and transfer to a plate.

3. In a bowl, mix remaining lemon zest with 1 tablespoon salt or more to taste.

4. Garnish zucchini with lemon salt before serving.

Grilled Onion Bites

This is a simple dish that takes only 30 minutes to make. Wrapped in foil and cooked on the grill, beef bouillon and butter are what give this sweet onion an incredible flavor.

Serves: 4 – Preparation Time: 5 minutes – Cooking Time: 25 minutes

Nutritional facts per serving: calories 96, total fat 8 g, saturated fat 5 g, carbs 6 g, sugar 4 g, fibers 1 g, protein 1 g, sodium 270 mg

Ingredients

1 sweet onion, peeled and end removed

⅓ stick butter, sliced into small pats

1 beef bouillon cube, crushed

Preparation

1. Preheat grill to 400 °F.

2. Take onion and slice in half but leaving about ¼ on the bottom unsliced. Slice lengthwise and diagonally in the same manner.

3. Sprinkle crushed bouillon cube all over onion, then place butter in between onion slits. Next, put onion on a sheet of aluminum foil and wrap completely. Twist the excess foil at the top to seal.

4. Transfer foil-wrapped onion onto grill and cook for about 25 minutes until onions are tender all the way through. Remove from grill.

5. Open up foil wrap and baste onion with any remaining butter and bouillon.

6. Serve.

Campsite Poutine

Tasty French fries slathered with a delicious DIY gravy and melted mozzarella cubes, this grilled dish makes a perfect snack for any time of the day.

Serves: 4 – Preparation Time: 15 minutes – Cooking Time: 30 minutes

Nutritional facts per serving: calories 817, total fat 43 g, saturated fat 18 g, carbs 87 g, sugar 2 g, fibers 8 g, protein 24 g, sodium 1385 mg

Ingredients

2 tablespoons unsalted butter, softened

1 large shallot, finely chopped

Pinch salt, plus more to taste

2 tablespoons all-purpose flour

2 cups beef stock

1 teaspoon Worcestershire sauce

1 teaspoon Dijon mustard

Ground black pepper, to taste

2 pounds frozen steak fries

2 tablespoons unsalted butter, melted

8 ounces fresh mozzarella, cut into small cubes

Fresh chives

Preparation

1. First, prepare the gravy by melting butter in a pot over medium heat of the camping grill. Add shallots and sauté for 2 to 3 minutes until tender. Sprinkle salt to season.

2. In the same pot, mix in flour and cook for about 1 minute until mixture turns light brown. Next, while stirring, pour in beef stock until mixture is well blended and smooth. Let

169

simmer until thick. Stir in Worcestershire sauce and mustard. Adjust seasoning by adding some salt and pepper, to taste. Reduce heat to low and keep warm.

3. Preheat grill to medium-high heat.

4. Lay out 2 large sheets of aluminum foil and put ½ frozen fries onto the center of each. Lightly pour 1 tablespoon melted butter over top of each. Fold up the sides of the sheet to create a packet. Seal tightly.

5. Transfer packets to camping grill. Cook for 10 minutes on each side, flipping once.

6. Open the packets and distribute mozzarella evenlyover the top of the fries. Cover grill and cook for 5 to 7 minutes more until mozzarella begins to melt.

7. To finish, add a drizzle of prepared gravy over the cheese and cover grill for just a few more minutes to heat through.

8. Remove from heat and sprinkle fresh chives on top. Serve.

Peanut Butter Tart Apple Crunchy Snacks

If you want a snack that's just as quick and easy to eat as it is to prepare, then this delicious peanut butter- and cereal-coated apple snack is the perfect one for you.

Serves: 2 – Preparation Time: 5 minutes – Cooking Time: 0 minutes

Nutritional facts per serving: calories 188, total fat 12 g, saturated fat 3 g, carbs 17 g, sugar 12 g, fibers 4 g, protein 6 g, sodium 111 mg

Ingredients

1 granny smith apple, cored

3 tablespoons peanut butter

½ cup preferred cereal

Preparation

1. Cut apples into ¼-inch thick slices.

2. Onto 1 side of each apple ring, layer a spread of peanut butter and sprinkle of your preferred cereal.

3. Serve.

About the Author

Louise Davidson is an avid cook who likes simple flavors and easy-to-make meals. She lives in Tennessee with her husband, her three grown children, her two dogs, and the family's cat, Whiskers. She loves the outdoor and has mastered the art of camp cooking on open fires and barbecue grills.

In colder months, she loves to whip up some slow cooker meals, and uses her favorite cooking tools in her kitchen, the cast iron pans, and Dutch oven. She also is very busy preparing Christmas treats for her extended family and friends. She gets busy baking for the holiday season sometimes as early as October. Her recipes are cherished by everyone who has tasted her foods and holiday treats.

Louise is a part-time writer of cookbooks, sharing her love of food, her experience, and her family's secret recipes with her readers.

She also loves to learn and share tips and tricks to make life a breeze.

More Books by Louise Davidson

Here are some of Louise Davidson's other cookbooks. You can click on the covers to take a look at any of them. You can also visit her author's page here: https://www.amazon.com/Louise-Davidson/e/B00MD2U4S6/ref=dp_byline_cont_pop_ebooks_1

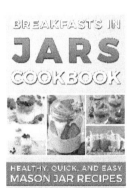

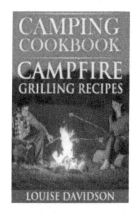

Appendix

Internal Temperature Cooking Charts

Beef, Lamb, Roasts, Pork, Veal, Ham

Rare	120 – 130°F (49 – 54°C)
Medium Rare	130 – 135°F (54 – 57°C)
Medium	135 – 145°F (57 – 63°C)
Medium Well	145 – 155°F (64 – 68°C)
Well Done	155°F and greater (68°C)

Pork, ribs

Fully Cooked	190 – 205°F (88 – 96°C)

Poultry

Fully Cooked	At least 165°F (74°C)

Fish

Fully Cooked	At least 130°F (54°C)

Barbecue Grilling Times

BEEF	Size	Grilling Time	Internal Temperature in °F (Fahrenheit)
Steaks	3/4" thick	3 to 4 min/side 4 to 5 min/side	Medium rare 145 Medium 160
Kabobs	1 inch cubes	3 to 4 min/side	145 to 160
Hamburger patties	1/2" thick	3 min/side	160
Roast, rolled rump (indirect heat)	4 to 6 lbs.	18 to 22 min/lb.	145 to 160
Sirloin tip (indirect heat)	3 1/2 to 4 lbs.	20 to 25 min/lb.	
Ribs, Back	cut in 1 rib portions	10 min/side	160
Tenderloin	Half, 2 to 3 lbs. Whole, 4 to 6 lbs.	10 to 12 min/side 12 to 15 min/side	Medium rare 145 Medium 160

PORK	Size	Grilling Time	Internal Temperature in °F (Fahrenheit)
Chops, bone in or boneless	3/4" thick 1 1/2" thick	3 to 4 min/side 7 to 8 min/side	145
Tenderloin	1/2 to 1 1/2 lbs.	15 to 25 min. total	145
Ribs (indirect heat)	2 to 4 lbs.	1 1/2 to 2 hrs.	145
Patties, ground	1/2" thick	4 to 5 min/side	145

HAM	Size	Grilling Time	Internal Temperature in °F (Fahrenheit)
Fully cooked (indirect heat)	any size	8 to 10 min/lb.	140
Cook before eating (indirect heat)	Whole, 10 to 14 lbs. Half, 5 to 7 lbs. Portion, 3 to 4 lbs.	10 to 15 min/lb. 12 to 18 min/lb. 30 to 35 min/lb.	160

179

LAMB Size		Grilling Time	Internal Temperature in °F (Fahrenheit)
Chops, shoulder, loin, or rib	1" thick	5 min/side	145 to 160
Steaks, sirloin, or leg	1" thick	5 min/side	145 to 160
Kabobs	1" cubes	4 min/side	145 to 160
Patties, ground	4 oz., 1/2" thick	3 min/side	160
Leg, butterflied	4 to 7 lbs.	40 to 50 min. total	145 to 160

VEAL Size		Grilling Time	Internal Temperature in °F (Fahrenheit)
Chops, steaks	1" thick	5 to 7 min/side	145 to 160
Roast, boneless (indirect heat)	2 to 3 lbs.	18 to 20 min/lb.	145 to 160

180

CHICKEN	Size	Grilling Time	Internal Temperature in °F (Fahrenheit)
Whole (indirect heat), not stuffed	3 to 4 lbs. 5 to 7 lbs. 4 to 8 lbs.	60 to 75 min. 18 to 25 min.lb. 15 to 20 min/lb.	165 to 180 as measured in the thigh
Cornish hens	18 to 24 oz.	45 to 55 min.	
Breast halves, bone in	6 to 8 oz. each	10 to 15 min/side	165 to 170
boneless	4 oz. each	7 to 8 min./side –	
Other parts:	4 to 8 oz.	10 to 15 min/side	165 to 180
Legs or thighs	4 oz.	8 to 12 min/side	
Drumsticks Wings,	2 to 3 oz.	8 to 12 min/side	

TURKEY	Size	Grilling Time	Internal Temperature in °F (Fahrenheit)
Whole turkey (indirect heat)	8 to 12 lbs.	2 to 3 hrs.	165 to 180 as measured in the thigh
	12 to 16 lbs.	3 to 4 hrs.	
	16 to 24 lbs.	4 to 5 hrs.	
Breast, bone in **boneless**	4 to 7 lbs.	1 to 1 3/4 hrs.	165 to 170
	2 3/4 to 3 1/2 lbs.	12 to 15 min/side	
Thighs, drumsticks (indirect heat) **Direct heat (precook 1 hr.)**	8 to 16 oz.	1 1/2 to 2 hrs. 8 to 10 min/side	165 to 180
Boneless turkey roll (indirect heat)	2 to 5 lbs.	1 1/2 to 2 hrs.	165 to 175
	5 to 10 lbs.	2 to 3 1/2 hrs.	

182

Tips for successful and safe barbecuing:

- To make sure that harmful bacteria, sometime present in uncooked meat and poultry, are destroyed during the cooking process, you must make sure that the internal temperature is high enough for safe consumption. Always use a meat thermometer inserted in the thickest part without touching any bones. Research from the U.S. Department of Agriculture (USDA) states that the color of the meat is not a dependable indicator meat or poultry has reached a temperature high enough to destroy harmful bacteria that may be present.
- Follow this chart for approximate cooking times, Outdoor grills can vary in heat.
- Use barbecue sauce during the last 15 to 30 minutes of grilling to prevent excess browning or burning resulting from the sugars of the sauce.
- USDA recommends cooking pork, beef, veal, lamb chops, ribs and steaks until it reaches a minimum internal temperature of 145°F and then let rest at least 3 minutes before slicing or consuming.
- Although it is safe to eat poultry with an internal temperature of 165°F, the flavors and the texture are best when the internal temperature reaches 170°F to 180°F

Source: Food Safety and Inspection Service, USDA

Cooking Conversion Charts

Measuring Equivalent Chart

Type	Imperial	Imperial	Metric
Weight	1 dry ounce		28g
	1 pound	16 dry ounces	0.45 kg
Volume	1 teaspoon		5 ml
	1 dessert spoon	2 teaspoons	10 ml
	1 tablespoon	3 teaspoons	15 ml
	1 Australian tablespoon	4 teaspoons	20 ml
	1 fluid ounce	2 tablespoons	30 ml
	1 cup	16 tablespoons	240 ml
	1 cup	8 fluid ounces	240 ml
	1 pint	2 cups	470 ml
	1 quart	2 pints	0.95 l
	1 gallon	4 quarts	3.8 l
Length	1 inch		2.54 cm

* *Numbers are rounded to the closest equivalent*

Oven Temperature Equivalent Chart

T(°F)	T(°C)
220	100
225	110
250	120
275	140
300	150
325	160
350	180
375	190
400	200
425	220
450	230
475	250
500	260

* $T(°C) = [T(°F)-32] * 5/9$
** $T(°F) = T(°C) * 9/5 + 32$
*** *Numbers are rounded to the closest equivalent*

Made in the USA
Columbia, SC
16 July 2020

13972602R00108